Syamal Gupta, Imperial College alumni, served the Tata Group. He joined TISCO as an engineering trainee and eventually rose to be director of Tata Sons. He led Tata Precision Industries, Singapore, and later Tata Exports, where he promoted several international joint ventures and new businesses in Africa. His accomplishments earned him several national and international awards and distinctions.

At the time of retirement, he was director of Tata Sons, and chairman of Tata International Ltd, Tata Elxsi, Tata Consulting Engineers, Tata Advance Material and Tata BP Solar. At present, he is a trustee at Tata Medical Centre Trust and is also Honorary Consul of the Republic of Namibia.

Dear Clare & Eric
Sending here a copy of my long
awaited & delayed book covering
my life story & 55 years with
Tatas. Imperial played a big role
in my life and your contribution
augments in my professional
development. I will savour a life
long friendship with both of you
with my compliments
Syamal Gupta

QUINTESSENTIALLY
TATA

MY JOURNEY OVER
55 SUMMERS

SYAMAL GUPTA

RUPA

Published by
Rupa Publications India Pvt. Ltd 2020
7/16, Ansari Road, Daryaganj
New Delhi 110002

Sales Centres:
Allahabad Bengaluru Chennai
Hyderabad Jaipur Kathmandu
Kolkata Mumbai

ISBN: 978-93-89967-18-0

First impression 2020

10 9 8 7 6 5 4 3 2 1

The moral right of the author has been asserted.

Printed in Parksons Graphics Pvt. Ltd, Mumbai

To my Mentors
Sumant Moolgaokar
and
Hugh Ford
for their guidance and kindness
over the years.

CONTENTS

Foreword by Ratan Tata   ix

Preface   xi

1. Early Days: First Breath at TISCO   1

2. Interlude: Assignment Europe   21

3. Home Again   38

4. Taking Charge in Singapore   61

5. Going International   104

6. The Africa Story   125

7. Strategic Alliances and Associations   152

8. League of Leadership   175

Epilogue   181

Acknowledgements   183

Index   185

FOREWORD

Mr Sumant Moolgaokar was well known for his tremendous capability of identifying promising technology. He was also known for his ability to identify individuals in the companies he headed, based on his intuitive assessment of individuals. Very often, his choice of persons would be surprising to others. But as it turned out he was seldom wrong.

Mr Syamal Gupta was one such person who Sumant Moolgaokar picked for his innovative and technical capability. Syamal Gupta was a young engineer in Tata Steel, well respected but rather obscure until he began interacting with Mr Moolgaokar. Syamal distinguished himself by developing plastic coated coloured sheets to replace conventional galvanized corrugated roofing sheets. This led to his being given leadership roles in several engineering projects in Tata Steel.

Syamal was subsequently selected by Mr Moolgaokar in the '70s to head the Tata Group's investments in technology in the Republic of Singapore in cooperation with the Singapore government. Syamal headed Tata Precision Industries which produced precision stampings for lead frames used in the semiconductor industry. Over those years, Syamal built unbelievable bonds of mutual respect with senior government officials.

Later, Syamal was recalled to India to head the growth of the Tata Group globally. He became the managing director and CEO of Tata Exports where he opened markets for Tata products in several African countries as also in South-East Asia and Europe. During these years, Syamal built bridges between the various new governments in the region, which resulted in the Tata Group being one of the more prominent exporters of goods and services in India.

Syamal retired from the Tata Group in 2009 as a member of the apex board of Tata Sons. These memoirs recount his memories of his years in the Tata Group and the growth of a young engineer's lifetime employment and his meritorious career within the Group over the years.

Ratan J. Tata

Ratan N. Tata
March, 2020

PREFACE

I spent 55 glorious years of service with the Tata Group. When some friends and colleagues suggested that I capture in a book the highlights of my career, I did not at first think it would be so daunting a task. It was only after I got down to working on the book that I discovered it was not going to be easy.

A lot had changed over the last half century. People had changed, society had evolved, businesses had transformed, governments had changed, and even countries. The world had undergone a metamorphosis. Nothing was as it had been when I first stepped into the portals of India's biggest business group, the House of Tatas.

Yet, as I reflected over the past five decades, I noticed a common thread right from the time of Jamsetji Tata through my time with the Group. This was the spirit of pioneering, the courage to go where none had ventured before and the determination to succeed which are all very alive even today. The Tata Group provided many firsts to the country, even to the world. Tatas always lead from the front.

'That's it!' I said to myself. The book would talk about the pioneering values at Tatas—how it inspires 'Leadership with a Difference' by seeding values and encouraging entrepreneurs and learning.

I joined Tata Iron and Steel Company in 1955, after my graduation in mechanical engineering, with the ambition simply to work as a good engineer. During my years, I had the privilege of working alongside Ratan Tata, former chairman and chairman emeritus of Tata Sons and other leaders in the Tata Group. Even after I formally retired as director, Tata Sons, in 2009, I have stayed associated with the Group.

There are few professional managers who work to serve a single institution for half a century—I am one of those. When people asked me how a man could work for a single organization his entire life, I had only one answer, 'Tatas as an organization simply grows on you.' A similar question was again asked of me at a Presidential Convention in Uganda in July 2009, in the presence of a number of Heads of State. I could only respond, 'Sir, the thing is that I do not know whether I belong to the Tatas or the Tatas belong to me!'

This then is the story of how the Tata Group went on to shape the thoughts and actions of one humble engineer and inspired him to lead the Tata way—thinking anew, carving pathways for others to follow, taking on myriad challenges and touching lives along the way. The book offers readers the story of how the Tatas entered high tech sectors, broke ground in new geographies and established new ventures around the world—told through a multitude of anecdotes and a little bit of history.

Nothing would bring me greater joy than to know that this book is a source of inspiration for readers, in some measure, however small, to 'Lead with a Difference', so that we may all leave behind a different world, free of environmental pollution and the effects of global warming, a world which is more peaceful, healthier and happier.

Chapter 1

EARLY DAYS: FIRST BREATH AT TISCO

I was born in a close knit family that ingrained in me values like diligence, integrity and the importance of education. My father was a sincere, honest and dedicated person. A distinguished man, he served as a gazetted officer in the West Bengal state government. He authored a number of law books related to the Land Settlement Act and other related topics, which served as reference material. I remember when he would wake up every day at 4 a.m. and do some physical exercise and thereafter, study and write notes for his books. He toiled hard in preparing his manuscripts. It was largely due to his position and his association with well-read people, that I had access to many highly educated and well-placed individuals.

As my father was in a job that was transferable, we frequently travelled from place to place. Following his transfer from Behrampur in the early 1940s, we moved into our new house in Calcutta (now Kolkata). Our neighbourhood boasted of doctors, engineers, chartered accountants, barristers and an actuary—a gentleman who belonged to our ancestral village. It was a time when business professionals like actuaries were rare. Additionally, we had a High Court judge, a professor of economics from Presidency College—all in our neighbourhood. We often lamented that although Calcutta had produced some of India's finest artists, writers and musicians, they were absent in our locality.

These were the early years of Independence and a period of struggle for the people of West Bengal in many ways. The Partition had taken a heavy toll, people were without a proper home or hearth, and there was scarcity of food and other essential items. Families were displaced, creating an overwhelming refugee crisis in our newly constituted country. Our family too was affected by the Partition. Many of our relatives came from across the border and stayed with us in our crowded home in Calcutta.

We were eight siblings—four brothers and four sisters. Our mother, mild-mannered and humble by nature, was a pillar of strength. She read books on a variety of subjects and shared with us a lot of common knowledge and wisdom. Her care and grooming contributed greatly to our early growth, education and career. She patiently managed the house and our daily needs, as well as those of the displaced family, with the resources available at her disposal post-Partition.

While this was a difficult time for us, we enjoyed staying together with our relatives, who had nowhere else to go. Until they gradually moved to their new homes over a period of two years, the elders slept on available beds while the young ones occupied bedrolls on the floor. This taught us to share and adjust with others while continuing our studies and sports. Whatever difficulties we encountered, we faced them unitedly.

Technology Education to Ignite Minds

The year 1951 was a stepping stone to determine my future course of studies to build a strong foundation towards a professional life. Having passed my intermediate science examination, opportunities of higher education lay before me in the field of arts, medicine, engineering and commerce. Intense discussions with my father and brothers about the available options and my strengths and inclination finally guided me to opt for my field of interest.

The country's newly acquired freedom had infused a spirit of nationalistic fervour among the youth of that time, further driven by a burning desire to do something new to build a strong and resilient India. I was offered admission in two major engineering colleges in Calcutta—Jadavpur and Shibpur. The College of Engineering and Technology (CET), the precursor to Jadavpur University, was created by the National Council of Education (NCE), a body formed to promote self-reliance and rebuild India through its educational system. The college was shifted to Jadavpur, near Calcutta in 1942 and was granted university status only in December 1955.

I decided to join CET, Jadavpur, to pursue my interest in mechanical engineering. Its engineering course was structured on the semester system, which was then, new in India. We spent the first two years studying the basics, like most engineering students across the world do even today. Jadavpur University had a good workshop—a machine shop with a number of milling, turning and grinding machines, a foundry, forge and carpentry shop, and we had to go through a number of electrical and mechanical engineering laboratories as part of our basic training. Though there were no computers in those days, we did have a course on mathematical computation. Interestingly, in addition to our technical courses, we had to do courses in humanities and the liberal arts. There was modern history, business English, industrial administration, costing and economics. As the size of each class was quite small, we became well-acquainted with each other. Many of my classmates were from different parts of India.

After four long years, our final year examinations concluded and it dawned on us that we were about to embark on different journeys. With some melancholy, we began to hang around the college, met in the college canteen or in the student hostel, had group singing sessions or went to the cinema together. There was much nostalgia when we exchanged our postal addresses and promised to remain in touch with each other.

> The highest of all pleasures is the feeling that we have added something, however small it may be, to the sum of human knowledge, of having assisted, even if only a little, the progress of humanity.
>
> To the graduates of this University all I have to say is you are fortunate that you live in a time of great challenges and great opportunities of achievement, which were not given at any other previous period of history. History is being made at greater speed than ever before, and if we are willing to make the effort, we can help history.
>
> —Excerpt from the speech by Dr Sarvepalli Radhakrishnan
> at the maiden convocation of Jadavpur University,
> 18 March 1956

I still recall my convocation with pride. It was Jadavpur University's maiden convocation and Dr S. Radhakrishnan, then vice president of India, delivered the inaugural speech. A renowned professor and a teacher of the highest calibre, he later went on to become the president of India. It was a matter of great pride to receive our degree in his presence. This occasion was also special as it marked the day when Jadavpur University was formally inaugurated by

Dr B.C. Roy, the first vice chancellor and also the chief minister of West Bengal.

This memorable event in our lives unfolded against a backdrop of India's recently won freedom from the British rule when the atmosphere was charged with nationalistic fervour. Patriotism ran high. As Indians, proud of their rich heritage, graduating students were expected to lead the country with their human values intact.

While many of my classmates were planning to go abroad for further studies and training, a few contemplated starting a small-scale industry. The rest of us started looking for job opportunities.

Barely a decade after Independence and the Partition of India, Calcutta was still dealing with its own crisis of thousands of displaced people pouring in from across the border looking for job security and livelihood. It was a time when the country was gearing up for an industrial revolution as envisaged by Prime Minister Pandit Jawaharlal Nehru. There was great euphoria about major government projects being enthusiastically initiated across India. Three major public-sector steel plants were being set up in the mid-1950s in Rourkela, Bhilai and Durgapur with German, Soviet and British assistance respectively. The government of India had also invested in other public-sector corporations like the Fertilizer Corporation of India, the Damodar Valley Corporation and the Heavy Engineering Corporation in Ranchi, besides making significant outlays in Bharat Heavy Electricals. To support the rebuilding of India, Indian Iron & Steel Company (IISCO) and Tata Iron and Steel Company (TISCO), both in the private sector, were also planning major expansion programmes.

Stepping into the Tata Fold

I kept in touch with some of my classmates to discuss our placement progress. We were young and ready to conquer the world. For an interview with a department of the government of West Bengal for a water distribution project funded by World Bank, I went attired in my father's jacket, feeling particularly confident. During the course of the interview, I was quizzed by the chief engineer while one of the seniors on the panel advised me that as a fresher, I should target industries in the private or public sectors, essentially to gain hands-on experience in design and manufacturing. It was strong and sound advice.

Amidst various job opportunities, I also received an interview call from TISCO, Jamshedpur, following a three-hour drawing test. I was interviewed by a panel headed by Paul Mueller, chief engineer of the company. Mueller particularly questioned me on hydraulics.

I was amongst the 15 young engineers finally selected by TISCO. I discussed these offers at home with my parents and brother and we decided that I should join it, considering steel and heavy industries were going to be the focus of India's growth story.

◆

I joined TISCO as a trainee in its Central Engineering and Development Department (CEDD) in September 1955. It was my first job, and Jamshedpur—my first move away from home. I had mixed feelings of apprehension and excitement and was a little overwhelmed by TISCO's reputation. We knew that the steel industry was growing fast and there would be great opportunities, but along with great expectations there was also great pressure.

As I walked into TISCO on my first day, with the confident gait of a 22 year old, little did I know that these would be my first steps to a journey of 55 years with the Tata Group; little could I envisage it would take me where it did.

As trainees, we were given a brief on the company and CEDD which had Design, Project Engineering, Electrical Engineering,

Construction, Inspection and other departments, and had a strength of about 3,000 people. Our batch of 15 engineers was first assigned to the design office.

While the CEDD Office was huge, fully air-conditioned and in immaculate condition, the design office was located in an old general office that only had fans and no air conditioning. There were huge stacks of drawings wherever one looked.

Once, J.R.D. Tata, chairman of Tata Sons for 52 years (1938–1991), was to visit the design office. Known for his penchant for orderliness, neatness and cleanliness at the workplace, a massive cleaning exercise was immediately undertaken with old drawings being removed and old papers being shoved into other departments. The de-cluttering was intended to be temporary and meant to last only till JRD's visit was over. As luck would have it, JRD expressed a desire to advance his visit to the design office that very afternoon, before the clean-up could be completed. As he took a tour and spoke to the staff, he noticed the mess that the design office was. The next thing everybody knew was that Tata had sanctioned setting up the new CEDD!

JRD was a perfectionist with an eye for detail. By nature, he was compassionate and wholeheartedly believed in taking care of his employees. The immediate outcome of his decision was that work efficiency in the design division went up significantly.

It was this same CEDD Office, which gave me tremendous insight into basic engineering. Working here amongst committed professionals was a humbling experience with the realization of just how much there was to learn! TISCO and Jamshedpur had much to offer. I was keen to make my work in this steel company a success, learn more about steel making and also learn about the history of the company.

Training for Life

We were one of the early batches of engineering graduates to be inducted into the training scheme at CEDD. The first assignment threw us completely off-balance. For a period of two to three weeks, we were to singularly concentrate on writing the letters A, B, C, D in both upper case as well as in lower case. Unbelievable! Graduates from premier engineering institutes were being made to write A, B, C, D as part of their training? Surely, we were groomed for bigger things! Disappointed as we were, we continued to write diligently. As we progressed, we discovered that we were gradually writing more carefully and neatly.

The chief draughtsman, P.K. Chatterjee, came around the drawing boards, observing everyone and keeping track of what was happening with the 200 draughtsmen working in the design office. One of the first jobs assigned to me was to draft a small walking bridge over the sheet bar and billet mill roller table, for which I was told to use the available steel from our store. I studied a whole lot of standard sketches and succeeded in drafting a staircase, fabricated as a bridge to cross over the roller tables. When it was finally fabricated and erected, I was elated with my first creation, even though this was a simple structure that a welder or a fitter could have created without a drawing.

With the high demand for steel and its short supply, TISCO had planned capacity expansion to two million tonnes of raw steel per annum in 1954. Kaizer Engineers of Oakland, California, was appointed as the consultant for the development and implementation of the expansion programme, to cost about ₹50 crore (₹500 million). The project was to be completed in 30 months.

CEDD design engineers and Works Department, all worked together in finalizing a blueprint for the major expansion programme. Those were hectic days for TISCO and Kaizer Engineers, but more so for the CEDD engineers who were also deeply involved with the project, and the most exciting days of my life. All of us were charged with a zealous fever and I was keen to utilize the opportunity for maximum results. TISCO had pioneering steel making expertise and we witnessed many technological breakthroughs, though there were many problems too.

The German company, Maschinenfabrik Sack GmBH, a reputed rolling mill builder, had designed, fabricated and supplied the Medium and Light Structural Mill to TISCO for its expansion programme. This was a cross-country mill with four stands at the end of the production line that produced angles, channels, beams and other light steel sections for continuous rolling. This meant that the steel could be rolled through different stages through the stands. Maschinenfabrik Sack had then deputed Emile Kersting as the commissioning engineer responsible for the erection and commissioning of the Mill to its rated capacity and for handing it over to TISCO. Kersting stayed in TISCO over three years.

However, this was the first time for Sack to design this particular type of mill and had no previous experience in continuous rolling of sections. Thus, while the round and flat products were produced without any problem, there were serious issues with the production of angles, I-beams and channels on continuous rolling. There were other technical issues too, in terms of roll pass, design and differential cooling of the section, flow of material, speed of rolling, guides and guards. I learnt that getting quality products at rated capacity, as per the schedule drawn at the time of placing the order, was a tough call.

The master roll turner, S. Dasgupta, renowned for having mastered the art of roll pass design, would often request me to calculate the volume of the products at different stages—significant for the final products—and also to find out the pattern of flow of material in different parts of the sections. This opportunity gave me a lot of exposure to the mechanics of rolling, roll pass design, flow of material, operation and quality control. I was constantly learning and that was a major source of satisfaction for me. I would often go beyond the call of duty, merely out of self-interest. However, even though much effort was put into formulating modifications, many of the sections could not be produced and alternative schedules had to be created.

Desire, When You Deserve

After three years of experience in the design office, a few of us were offered jobs in the Projects Department in view of the company's massive expansion programme. The new job offered a ₹40–50 raise in salary per month besides other benefits, which was big money in those days. A lot of people opted for the change. However, a few of us wanted to continue in the drawing office to gain more experience in design and drafting. I felt it was prudent to stick to the design office, compromising on the salary, until I switch to a project or construction job. This, I think, was my first major career decision.

In 1958, some of my friends informed me that a British company was looking for young engineers with experience and knowledge in rolling mills, who would be trained in their design office and Works in London. This seemed like a rare opportunity that could fulfil my dreams of going to London and seeing the world—a dream nurtured by many youth of my time. Even my brothers had moved overseas, to the UK and the United States of America (US), for post-graduate studies.

I applied for the job and was shortlisted to meet the chairman at the company's Calcutta Head Office for a final meeting. Following the interview, I was given an offer letter. Imagine my joy as I read it! The training was to be in England at their design office and manufacturing centre. The letter also stated that I would have to leave immediately and they would assist in organizing my passport and other formalities. On my return to India, they would offer me a salary of ₹1,100 per month, a car and a three-bedroom bungalow!

It was an unimaginable offer and I simply could not believe it was all happening to me! This was an opportunity of a lifetime and I was just 25 years old. I was thrilled and excited about going to London and rushed home with the letter of appointment.

Celebrations were on for a wedding in the family but I managed to take my mother aside and break the news about going to London. She knew how my generation aspired to be in London and said she was very happy for me. Then I approached my father with the offer letter. He too was happy that I had been offered such a tempting job, but said the salary offered by the British company was unrealistic for a man of my age and experience. 'Desire, when you deserve,' he said. Such salaries were paid those days to chief engineers close to their retirement. He was apprehensive about it and felt I was making a hasty decision. He was keen that I continue working in a great organization like TISCO. What he said made a deep impact on me. I turned down the offer and returned to Jamshedpur and focused on my job at TISCO.

A few weeks later, my immediate boss, D.V. Rao, told me that Mueller wanted to meet me and that I should immediately go to the office of the chief design engineer, H.P. Bodhanwala, who would brief me and take me to the chief engineer's office. He was worried and so were the people who overheard him. The whole office became tense and apprehensive. I was bewildered and all sorts of fearful thoughts crossed my mind as I followed Bodhanwala to Mueller's office.

What transpired in the meeting took me totally by surprise. After exchanging a few pleasantries, Mueller came straight to the point. He was aware that I had been offered another good job but chose to remain with TISCO. I was worried I would lose my job, but my fears were unfounded. Mueller expressed happiness that I decided to stay back at TISCO. 'If you young people go away, then who will run TISCO?' he mused.

As part of TISCO's expansion programme, a new Inspection and Design (I&D) Department created in the Engineering division in 1956 to coordinate the activities was recruiting engineers. Bodhanwala and Chatterjee, who was now the assistant chief engineer, interviewed me for the position of an assistant engineer. Thereafter, I was selected to work in the I&D Department.

The appreciation and promotion by my seniors boosted my commitment towards the Tatas, and to TISCO in particular. I put my heart and soul into my new task and always go the extra mile to deliver more than expected. My parents too were happy that I had chosen to continue with TISCO. It was my first job and from then on, there was never an occasion when I wanted to leave the company for a better salary or for greater career opportunities elsewhere. The Tatas took great care of their people.

First Engineering Success

TISCO's modernization included a Sheet Bar and Billet Mill No. 2 (SBBM2) was designed, manufactured and supplied by the world-famous rolling mill builder, Demag of West Germany. The mill that produced billets used in engineering industries, steel sheet bars for roofing and construction, and tin bars that were further processed into strips for containers, was installed and commissioned in November 1958. However, there were several serious shortcomings in the operation and production of tin bars in the mill.

The management was deeply concerned when the new rolling mill from a reputed world-class manufacturer like Demag, was not fully functional and causing loss of production. In view of the urgency, the technical director, Firoze Kutar, called a high-level meeting to find a solution for the trouble-free operation of the mill. I attended this meeting with the CEDD chief engineer, K.P. Mahalingam. While we were waiting outside the technical director's room, Sir Jehangir Ghandy, director-in-charge and the big boss of TISCO, Jamshedpur, happened to pass by. It was the first time I got a glimpse of him. He remarked, 'My God, such a high-powered meeting! So many people attending. What will this cost the company in time and money?' Though he said it in a light note, there was much to learn from it for a youngster like me.

It was my first opportunity to enter the office of the technical director. As I settled down and silently looked around, I noticed a poster behind his desk that read thus:

THERE WAS A JOB TO BE DONE. EXPERTS FROM ALL OVER THE WORLD CAME AND SAID IT COULD NOT BE DONE. THEN CAME A FOOL, AND HE DID THE JOB BECAUSE HE DID NOT KNOW THAT IT COULD NOT BE DONE.

I was mesmerized reading these lines and was in great awe at seeing all the top bosses around me. Shortly thereafter, a heated argument ensued within the group and I was shaken out of my stupor. Works blamed the Engineering Department and Demag's inability to resolve the problem. The Engineering Department was also investigating the matter that had also been referred to the Demag head office in Germany. I became deeply interested in studying the problem and devoted time to analyse the operations step-by-step—the layout, material flow and design of the piler, pinch roller and other auxiliaries. This posed a real challenge and I felt motivated to study it at length.

I was keen on resolving the problem and started developing various proposals to do so, finally zeroing in on one, which would ensure a smooth flow of materials directly to the tin bar cooling bed yard, involving just one operation instead of six. I approached my seniors in the Project Department—J.R. Sen, K.N. Venkat and J.C. Chakraborty. They were supportive and suggested that I place the proposal before the chief design engineer for his consideration.

I went to Bodhanwala and told him I had been working on the SBBM2 problem. 'I think we have a proposal that will address the problem,' I said. With a lot of hesitation and anxiety I spread out the revised layout and the modifications of the handling equipment. Bodhanwala examined the proposal closely and finally said, 'This is interesting.'

We then dashed to Mueller's office. Bodhanwala told him that there was a proposal for SBBM2's tin bar handling system, which would address all the issues. 'Syamal has worked out the proposal and it merits consideration,' he told Mueller.

Mueller, the celebrated chief engineer, glanced through the revised proposal and drawings, and started describing the process I had proposed without giving me a chance to explain. He could grasp the proposal very fast. Mueller's eyes sparkled and we could see he was excited that a viable solution had at last been found. I was told to prepare a note describing the proposal with the estimated capital cost and the time schedule.

It was decided that the proposal should be discussed at the highest level with Dr Hans Reuter, chairman of Demag, who was visiting Jamshedpur on 9 November 1960, and to seek his views. Records showed that a high-level meeting was held between Sir Ghandy and Dr Reuter, and the proposal was finally approved for implementation.

The company invested approximately ₹2 crore to implement the revised project proposal. Equipment was ordered immediately from Demag, Germany. It was a breakthrough and I was happy that the proposal had worked. Demag too was relieved that a suitable solution had been found and said they would be delighted to host me in Germany.

As a young engineer in my mid-twenties, with limited experience in the steel company, I had been hesitant to put up the proposal. For me, the problem posed an interesting challenge, which needed an urgent solution. The work culture prevalent in TISCO and the support of the top bosses were essential for the success of this project. Mahalingam went out of his way to support me in developing and implementing the project. He also brought me to the attention of the top management. Following the successful implementation of the proposal, Mueller sent a letter dated 6 October 1961, addressed to S.K. Nanavati, general manager, TISCO, an extract of which reads thus:

> Gupta is 28 years old, and is currently an Assistant Engineer working in the Project Department, having completed nearly seven years service with the Steel Company. He is one of our competent and enthusiastic engineers. In the process of evolving the proposal adopted, he spent considerable time diligently studying the problem from various angles, both on the drafting board as well as in the field, regardless of official duty hours. The interest, perseverance and enthusiasm that he has displayed, are commendable. The merits of the proposal he has put forward are unquestionable. Considering his junior status in the organisation and background of his relatively short experience in the Steel Company, the painstaking efforts he has put in and the results achieved call for special recognition.

The financial savings as a result of this proposal were estimated at approximately ₹37 lakh annually, when TISCO's profits were between ₹5 and ₹6 crore per annum. The modified version of the plant remained in operation for many years.

The whole exercise was interesting and I was engrossed in it without self-interest, not to mention that this project helped me get a prestigious Fellowship from the Institution of Mechanical Engineers (IMechE), London; later on from the Royal Academy of Engineering and Imperial College, London; and also the Indian National Academy of Engineers (INAE).

Nostalgia: TISCO Turns 50

Looking back at my early years in TISCO, I fondly recall the lighter moments. The major two-million tonne expansion programme of TISCO was complete and coincided with the company's Golden Jubilee. This occasion was celebrated on 3 March 1958 for which Prime Minister Pandit Jawaharlal Nehru accompanied by his daughter, Indira Gandhi, arrived in Jamshedpur as the guests of honour.

The whole township wore a festive look as Ustad Bismillah Khan's melodious shehnai (clarinet) played through the loudspeakers. Colourful arches and floral decorations embellished the route from the airport all the way to the Works, and people waved the national flag to welcome the prime minister.

Other government dignitaries who graced the occasion were: Morarji Desai, then union finance minister; Sardar Swaran Singh, central minister for steel; Dr Zakir Hussain, governor of Bihar; Dr S. Sinha, chief minister of Bihar and Edwina Mountbatten, wife of Lord Mountbatten, the last viceroy of India. Tata dignitaries present at the occasion were: J.R.D. Tata with his wife Thelma, Sir Jehangir Ghandy, Lady Ghandy and S.K. Nanavati, along with others from the top management of TISCO. A special commemorative stamp and a first-day cover were also issued by the Indian Posts and Telegraph Department.

On that day, Pandit Nehru inaugurated the newly commissioned Steel Melting Shop or SMS3 at TISCO that produced molten steel. From a distance of almost half a mile, we saw JRD, Thelma Tata, Nehru and Indira Gandhi heading towards the SMS3. Later, Nehru also visited the under-construction site of the new rolling mill. It was a moment of great joy and pride for all of us and the entire event is vividly etched in my mind to this day. That evening, as part of the celebrations, Nehru also inaugurated the new and beautifully designed Jubilee Park with the symbolic planting of a banyan sapling. He then proceeded to a podium erected at the park to unveil a huge newly installed statue of Jamsetji Tata, the founder of TISCO.

JRD spoke to the gathering at the park and said that it was felt the workers and their families needed a haven of rest and beauty and so, the company had decided to dedicate the beautiful park to the people of Jamshedpur.

A day prior to the inauguration of the park, Pheroze Tarapore, chief project engineer, had been developing a device to automate the unveiling of the Founder's statue. However, the device set up was not working satisfactorily and several alternatives had to be explored. There were no electronic gadgets or micro motors in those days. At that juncture, as the device was being tested, JRD arrived unscheduled to oversee the preparations. Tarapore had by then run out of options and explained to Tata that as a fall back arrangement, when the Prime Minister pushes the switch, a bell would sound and the boys behind the statue would manually draw up the curtains on hearing it.

JRD enquired, 'What will happen if the switch is pressed and the bell fails to ring? What will you do?' He then suggested with a straight face, 'Why don't you attach livewires to people operating the curtain so that when the switch is pressed, a mild current will give them an electrical shock and they will all drop down thus lifting the curtain without fail?' Well, JRD has his witty moments, and that helped to lighten the atmosphere. Soon, Tarapore sorted out the problem and the inauguration of the statue went without any glitches.

As I think of all the people who built Jamshedpur and this giant of a company, I cannot forget to mention the Santhals, the local tribal men and women, who have contributed in no small measure to the development of TISCO. The Santhals are a peaceful and friendly tribe. True to their traditions, they love to sing and dance on festive occasions, particularly on Poornima or full moon night. During winter months, we would take a bicycle ride out of town to Seraikella village to watch their famed Chhau dance. Their customs and their ways seemed pure and untouched by city culture. I remember them as a happy, healthy and hardworking people who worked to make TISCO what it is today.

Every year on 3 March, the entire Jubilee Park is lit up with lights and is resplendent with illuminated fountains to commemorate the birth anniversary of Jamsetji Nusserwanji Tata.

Fifty-one years later, on 3 March 2009, just prior to my retirement from Tata Sons and other Group companies, B. Muthuraman, managing director, Tata Steel, invited me to be the guest of honour and participate in the Annual Day function at Jamshedpur. I was deeply touched by this gesture and overwhelmed too, as I recalled being a participant in the parade when I was young.

Present at the function were Ratan Tata and other dignitaries. In the morning, I garlanded the Founder's statue at the Main Gate. As was the practice, Jubilee Park was lit up the whole week through. To my surprise, I was requested to inaugurate the evening function as well by switching on the lights and yes, the system was fully automated. With a mere push of the button, the lights came on and the fountains rose majestically. What a magnificent sight that was to behold! My mind raced back to March 1958 and I realized I had come full circle.

TISCO had grown from a two million tonnes per annum

capacity to 10 million tonnes per annum. It had also set up another green-field project for a steel plant in Odisha, with a capacity of three million tonnes per annum. In addition, TISCO has acquired British Steel in the UK to become the second largest steel producer in the world. The Tata Group had grown to US$100 billion under the leadership of Group Chairman Ratan Tata.

Going Overseas

Following completion of the two-million-tonne expansion programme at Jamshedpur, there was a lull on the job front for me. My passion for learning the basics of rolling was growing stronger. I now wanted to learn the calculation methods for roll force, torque, and spread for rolling mills. In those days, the making and shaping of steel and all that went into it was based more on experience rather than sound theoretical knowledge. I wanted to go beyond that; to go deeper into the theories of the rolling and wanted some sound experience in this area.

I decided to go to Germany, a country known for its engineering and scientific excellence and capabilities, along with its achievements in arts, literature and science. I already had a few contacts in Demag, Maschinenfabrik Sack and Schloemann—the three German rolling mill designers and builders. Two of these companies had already indicated that they would be happy to have me with them in Germany whenever I got the opportunity to go over.

Sometime in 1961–62, Dr Azbeck of Maschinenfabrik Sack was visiting Jamshedpur when I had met him and expressed a desire to take some time off in order to work in Germany. Maschinenfabrik Sack was a reputed company. They designed rolling mills and manufactured them in their own workshop. Dr Azbeck, on his return to Germany, sent me a letter inviting me to work in Maschinenfabrik Sack, Dusseldorf. I was pleased with the offer of a paid position and broached the subject with my wife and family who supported my decision. My wife wanted to stay with her parents and in-laws in Calcutta during my absence.

The company granted me study leave to the extent of leave due to me, plus leave without pay up to two years. But I had to make my own arrangements for my travel and stay abroad, and to personally bear all my expenses. I booked my ticket through Ashok Mukherjee who was the high-profile public relation officer of Tata Steel, Calcutta, a good sportsman, a great animal lover and a well-connected person. I got a good fare from Calcutta to Frankfurt, then to Dusseldorf for ₹1,400. The travel agent advised me that as my brother was in London, if I pay an additional ₹37, they would also throw in an onward ticket to London.

I finally bid goodbye to my friends in Jamshedpur on 30 November 1962, and left for Kolkata with my wife, Chandra. Coincidentally, that was the day Tata International was incorporated. Little did I know that one day I would return to the shores of India to be associated once again with this very company.

Chapter 2

INTERLUDE: ASSIGNMENT EUROPE

Following the call of learning, I flew out of India on 2 December 1962. With hope and confidence as my companions, I boarded an Air India flight from Calcutta to Frankfurt. Clearly, Air India in those days was a maharaja airline and they treated passengers like maharajas too! Not surprisingly, it was then ranked among the top three airlines of the world. JRD was its chairman and the standards demonstrated by the airline were remarkable. I landed early in the morning in Frankfurt only to be hustled into another aircraft to proceed to Dusseldorf.

On 3 December 1962, I landed in Dusseldorf where I was to start work with Maschinenfabrik Sack. As I stepped out of immigration, I was delighted to see a smiling Emile Kersting waving at me. I had known him from his time in India where he worked with TISCO and represented Maschinenfabrik Sack.

Kersting drove me to a hotel booked close to their office and spent some time recalling his days in Jamshedpur and settling me down in my new environment. The cold and misty Dusseldorf weather was anything but welcoming. Although I felt lonely and desolate in this new country, I was happy to be in Germany, the land that has given the world great people like Albert Einstein, Max Mueller and Karl Marx. I felt a childlike enthusiasm to be on this mission of discovery, and was amazed at the discipline and passion the Germans had for technology. The next morning, wrapped up in layers of warm clothing, I braved the cold and walked across the street to the Sack office. Kersting took me around the office, Works, and finally to the engineering and design office, which was big and accommodated 200 designers. They worked here with the manufacturing facilities right next door.

Over the next few days Kersting introduced me to Dr Sack, the chairman of the company and Dr Azbeck, the executive director, whom I already knew. The Azbeck and Sack families owned Maschinenfabrik Sack and had been in business for over two generations. Dr Sack, although past 75 years of age, would attend office every single day. I marvelled at his passion and commitment at his age.

According to Sack's research in those days, the growth of flat products for auto and white goods industry was the future. This gave me the opportunity to explore new trends in engineering steel rolling mills. Kersting discussed with me at length how best my time could be utilized at Sack. They were designing plate and wide strip mills with a capacity of 1 million tonnes, which was new those days. They believed that the steel industry will need to go for major expansion in India and TISCO too may grow significantly in the production of flat products. In this direction, my experience was of value to the company.

Maschinenfabrik Sack arranged for me to visit the continuous wide strip mill that they had built recently in Salzgitter to get first-hand knowledge of the high volume continuous strip mills. Those days, we did not have continuous strip mills in TISCO and

I thought it would be a logical choice to explore wide sheet mills. Of course, today, we have the best strip mill and flat products mill.

Living in Dusseldorf

Maschinenfabrik Sack soon found suitable accommodation for me to stay at Ratingen, a few miles away from Dusseldorf. This meant that the day started as early as 5.30 a.m. and I would walk 10 minutes to catch the 7 a.m. bus to work. Soon it was Christmas— my very first in Dusseldorf. They called it Wynette. On my way back from work, I walked around a bit to soak in the festive, wintry air. Stores were lit up and decorated and there was a general bustle and activity along the popular shopping areas. It reminded me of Diwali and Durga Puja back home in Kolkata.

One day, Kersting and I were having a cup of coffee, when he remarked, 'I hope you have met other people from your country. There are quite a few Indians living here in Germany.' He said I would be able to meet them at the Africa Asia Society where they all met every Saturday. I soon discovered there were several people from Jamshedpur living in Germany and I managed to connect with them.

There was also a bowling alley in the basement of the office. I was invited to take part in the game on Tuesday evenings. This gave me an opportunity to socialize with my colleagues. Everybody played the game and enjoyed a few rounds of drinks. I realized that this was a normal way of life and probably the weather too had something to do with it.

One day, at the bowling alley, I mentioned that I saw a certified barber at the salon. Kersting explained, 'Oh Gupta, please understand, in Germany you need to have a trade certificate or a degree in every profession. Everything you do, calls for a certificate.' I found that the Germans had a training school for all trades.

Perhaps this is why they excel in all that they do. I also came across a few young boys who went to an engineering school at night. In Germany, young people could get opportunities to train in the evenings as technicians while continuing to hold day jobs. They learnt how to draw, how to sketch and how to do the calculations. Ultimately, these students could choose to go to an engineering school or university for a degree. This, I thought, was a very good training programme. These ideas remained in incubation with me, to be recalled at a later time when I could put them to good use in my days at Tata Precision Industries (TPI), Singapore.

The Germans' pre-occupation with precision, neatness and accuracy for the smallest tasks never failed to impress me. If they placed a pencil on the table, they would do even that to perfection. They were always immaculately dressed, not expensively.

In Dusseldorf, one of our pastimes on Saturdays was to go to the downtown Jan-Wellem-Platz at the city centre. There was a well-appointed Air India office round the corner. Here, we browsed through Indian newspapers back to back. Air India also offered another great service—we could receive letters from home through them. That was our Air India of those days!

In 1963, I went to the Hanover Industrial Fair, one of the largest trade fairs in the world, with my friends. It was an experience to see so many people from all over the world come and display their products and capabilities. I hoped that someday, India and the Tatas too would showcase their products and services at the Fair. This vision came true years later in 1984, when I was with Tata Exports and the Tatas participated at this fair. We had a huge stall showcasing our engineering capabilities. The visit by Tata Sons directors—Sumant Moolgaokar, Russi Mody and Darbari Seth—along with other dignitaries to our stall clearly announced the Tatas had arrived on the international scene.

Draw of the Imperial

Around mid-1963, I decided to visit London to spend some time with my brother Kajal. He had gone to London much earlier and had joined the University of London as a doctoral student with a scholarship. Kajal occupied a room in a building owned by a Bangladeshi (person from former East Pakistan, now Bangladesh). There was an Indian restaurant downstairs and Kajal and a few other students lived upstairs.

During my short stay in London, Kajal went to great lengths discussing my future plans and advised me that if I intended to get into the fundamentals of applied mechanics, it would be wiser for me to take a course at a university. He took me through some relevant brochures and journals, got me to talk to his friends and even showed me around Imperial College which was one of the top science and engineering institutions. In those days, Imperial had the maximum number of Indians among its foreign students, which was around 150. I was motivated to apply for a two-year postgraduate course at Imperial College.

One day Kajal was showing me around London and as we were walking towards Buckingham Palace, I suddenly came upon an impressive office with the signboard TATA LIMITED. A Tata company right in front of Buckingham Palace! I was thrilled. I knew about Tata Limited and I remembered that Bill Hayles who was the Controller of Stores and Purchases (COP) in TISCO, Jamshedpur, had been transferred and appointed as executive director with Tata Limited, London. Trying not to think about my casual attire, I went into the office with my brother and called on Hayles. He was happy to receive us and as it turned out, he was aware that I was in Germany with Maschinenfabrik Sack on study leave. It was a good meeting. Eventually, I returned to Germany—this time by train, boat and bus.

Back in Germany, I started work again. One day, I received a letter from Imperial College offering me admission. I could not contain my happiness because the doors to further education had opened for me. Of course, it meant I would have to leave my job at Sack.

I informed my parents and my wife, Chandra, about the new development. My parents had always encouraged me to pursue higher education. Chandra, too, was understanding about my desire to take up this offer. I also informed my company that I had decided to go ahead and study. Dr Azbeck and Kersting too encouraged me to join Imperial College. Dr Azbeck said that their doors would always remain open for me to return at any time I wished. I was touched by the send-off party they arranged for me in the bowling alley where I had, in the past few months, spent many a pleasant evening with my colleagues. I started winding up in Dusseldorf and said goodbye to my colleagues, who were more like friends after 10 months in Germany.

Although receiving the admission letter from Imperial College was a dream come true, I soon realized there were other important matters that needed my attention, such as coping with the courses and financing my stay in London. When I settled my income tax, which took less than 10 minutes, to my surprise they refunded some money to me, which was a minor windfall.

I moved in with Kajal in Battersea, London, and managed to pay the fee of £75 for the first year. I also looked for suitable accommodation around the college, which was difficult to find as it was an upmarket area.

Imperial College is well known for its world-class research programmes and consistently ranks among the top 10 technical universities in the world. I joined Imperial College of Science & Technology, University of London, in September 1963 for the post graduate course in applied mechanics (plasticity). We were about

20 students in this discipline. The dean of engineering, Prof. Sir Owen Saunders, Fellow of the Royal Society (FRS), addressed the fresh postgraduate students and formally welcomed us. Course work started immediately.

After being away from academic life for more than seven years, I realized I needed to put in extra effort, much more than I had initially anticipated. There were new subjects in this course such as tensor calculus, quantum mechanics and finite element analysis, which I had never studied, but were relevant for solving problems in rolling (plasticity). All these subjects were highly mathematical and needed a good knowledge base. It was challenging and I had to put extra efforts to toil hard, although I almost gave up sometimes.

I am particularly grateful to Prof. Bickley, FRS, emeritus professor of mathematics. A few students, like me, who attended Imperial College after some industrial experience, were given the opportunity to brush up on their rusty mathematics as was usually the case, by taking additional classes. These classes were taken by Prof. Bickley. While he only had partial vision, his knowledge and compassion were remarkable. Whenever I approached him with problems, he took special care to ensure that I understood the subject. He was a great teacher and always kind and helpful to me and other students during our difficult times. I always remember him with respect.

Another time, when I was working on my research project on Hot Rolling at Imperial College, I was struck with some idea on grain growth and crystal structure that changes in the material in rolling. I thought this was a totally new idea. I was very excited and taking it forward, shared the idea with Prof. Hugh Ford, FRS, who was head of the Department of Mechanical Engineering. He calmly and quietly listened to me without interruption, then asked a few questions to guide me to the point where I realized my idea was totally wrong. He encouraged me to think. I felt disgusted about making a fool of myself and apologized to Prof. Ford. Years later when I met Prof. Ford, I recounted this particular interaction with him. But he appeared not to recollect it. He, however, said, 'One may drift, but our job is to encourage people to think and guide them in the right direction.' This positively influenced me.

Another noteworthy teacher was Prof. Grootenhuis, who encouraged us to find our own solutions. We were once doing an experiment on vibration in the laboratory. Prof. Grootenhuis would observe our progress from time to time. After working on the experiment for a few days, we were rather confused and at a loss for not having arrived at the correct results. The professor was encouraging. 'Please continue to work on this experiment, it could be the most interesting experience of your life, though you may not get the desired results,' he said. He sat alongside us for a couple of hours. He studied our line of approach, helped us to identify our mistakes and finally guided us to complete the experiment successfully.

Another thing I learnt was unassuming humility from eminent people. One day, sometime in 1964, I was at the Physics Department in the Senior Common Room waiting for a friend to join me. While I was having a cup of tea, I saw a sober looking gentleman walking towards me. Approaching me, he asked, 'May I join you, sir?' He sat down beside me sipping from his cup of tea and enquired about the work I was doing at the Mechanical Engineering Department. After he finished his tea, he wished me all the best, picked up his cup and saucer, and kept them on the rack.

In the meantime, I noticed my friend sitting quietly elsewhere in the room sipping his cup of tea. Just as I wondered why he did not join us, my friend walked up to me and enquired if I knew whom I had been talking to. He told me it was none other than Nobel Laureate Prof. Patrick Blackett, an experimental physicist, known for his work on cloud chambers, cosmic rays and palaeomagnetism.

What a noble, unassuming and humble person he was! There was just so much to learn from such eminent people.

Tata Funds My Education

After I had settled down at Imperial College, I got in touch with Bill Hayles at Tata Limited. He introduced me to Behram Saklatvala, the managing director of Tata Limited in London, who was a perfect gentleman and a nationalist Indian. Tata Limited often hosted top executives and directors visiting the UK, especially people from TISCO, Jamshedpur. Once, at the instance of Hayles, I visited the London Office to meet Mahalingam, chief engineer at CEDD, TISCO. Hayles took us to a corner restaurant for a meal, where Mahalingam expressed his happiness on my pursuing a course on plasticity. He said that this was a golden opportunity, beneficial to both me and the steel company. However, he expressed his displeasure that I had decided to take on this venture without tying up loose ends. 'Don't you think you should have been more responsible to yourself and the family?' he asked. He was aware of my difficulties in managing both responsibilities simultaneously.

On his return to Jamshedpur, Mahalingam met S.K. Nanavati, the then director-in-charge of TISCO, and strongly recommended sponsorship of my education at Imperial College. The management soon approved and my stay in London too was sanctioned.

Nearly half a century later, browsing through my collection of old letters, I came across a letter that Mahalingam had written to me in 2006 when I completed 50 years with the Tata Group. His letter touched my heart and brought back fond memories of my early engineering days. He had written:

My Dear Syamal,

I hope that my name still rings a bell! It truly warmed the cockles of my heart to see in the April 2006 issue of the Tata Review, the text and photographs of '50 Golden Years of the Quintessential Tata Man'. More so, as they evoked nostalgic memories of the years 1956–72, when I was plodding my way in Tata Steel's Central Engineering & Development Division to become the Chief Engineer with the pleasure of you working by my side, among others. The realisation that I had a small role to play in your spectacular progress in the House of Tata is most rewarding.

It is with a sense of pride and fulfilment that I recall the period 1962–65, when you went to Germany as a junior engineer and UK entirely on your own on 'Study Leave without pay', and all expenses had to be borne by you. On one of my business trips to London, when Bill Hayles, then Tata Ltd's Director and I were exchanging notes on Jamshedpur 'gossip', he told me all about your initial struggle and hard work to make both ends meet in London, going even to the extent of 'washing dishes' in restaurants and so on. Then and there, I decided to do my little bit as Chief Engineer for a most deserving staff member. You may recall that on my return, I had strongly recommended your case to the late S.K. Nanavati, then Tata Steel's Director-in-charge for entire reimbursement of your passage to and fro as well as payment of salary for the full period of two years and odd, while you were away, which were readily sanctioned by him. The financial strain on your personal resources was thus, relieved to a great extent at the time.

This funding support alleviated my situation and I put my heart and soul into my studies. I felt honoured to be a part of Tatas and grateful that they supported me in fulfilling my career goals and my stay requirements. By November 1963, I managed to find accommodation in South Kensington in London, closer to my college, which helped reduce the commuting time. For an occasional treat, I used to go to India House where one could get a decent Indian meal at a bargain price. My needs were few and I was content with life. I could pay for my accommodation, had enough for my meals at the college and managed with the weekly allowance of £5.50. Life was good. However, probably because of the way we were brought up, I was not an extrovert and it took me some time to make new friends. Once I got to know my classmates, I realized we were a good mix of students from the UK, Japan, India, Hong Kong, South America and other countries, and we would share many interesting stories. The group gelled well, so well in fact that one of our English classmates claimed each time he went home for the weekend, his mother could not understand his language anymore because it was laced with an international blend of chiefly Brazilian and Indian influences. Then to add to everybody's laughter, he said now that his mother had once again indoctrinated him in the Queen's English, he was finding it difficult to understand us!

At Imperial, a lot of research work was carried out in association with industry leaders like BEA, British Steel, Rolls Royce, Duropack, Bisra and many other organizations. These were also the nascent years of computers. We were taught languages like FORTRAN and COBOL, but soon a new digital computer, 360 B, was installed at the college that was accessible to everyone.

What Imperial taught us was the virtue of continual learning to keep abreast of technology. The courses were constantly being upgraded, working alongside industry which funded many of the research in universities those days. The College also continually promoted new research projects that ranged from steel to advanced materials, plastics, semi-conductors and automation.

Meeting My Guru

At the end of December 1963, after the first semester at Imperial College, a notice was put up listing research projects for higher degrees in the Mechanical Engineering Department. One of the projects was related to hot rolling of steel. I was excited. To study and research on the mechanics of rolling was the very purpose of my coming to Imperial College! I immediately applied for it.

Prof. Ford interviewed all prospective students and allocated research projects. He was particularly happy to note that I was from TISCO—he knew about TISCO from his association with British Iron and Steel Research Institute. Therefore, although he was only guiding postdoctoral students at the time, he decided to make an exception in my case, and immediately registered me to work with him on the calculation method of roll forces and torque in hot rolling. As a research supervisor, he was an excellent guide.

He broadly discussed the outline of the project and gave me a list of articles to read and books for references with the specific page numbers. I was to come back to him with a synopsis in three weeks. He also told me to utilize certain data on the project from the work done by Prof. G. Wallquist of the Royal Institute of Technology, Stockholm.

He brought me from the classroom into the laboratory and inducted me into research. His methods always remained subtle and gentle. His motivation was such that it rekindled my own desire to get into research & development (R&D) activities. Much later, in one of his letters, he wrote to tell me that I had an analytical bent of mind—an important quality of a good researcher. In addition to regular classes, I worked hard on my research project. The experience at TISCO helped me a great deal. When my work was completed, I submitted the draft of my dissertation to Prof. Ford for his comments and advice. I further made a presentation before the students and professors to defend my dissertation. Prof. Ford, Prof. Alexander and Prof. Grootenhuis, all stalwarts in their respective areas, attended my presentation. Prof. Ford expressed his pleasure with my research and presentation and I remember his commenting with an 'Excellent!' He suggested that we publish a paper together, based on my research project. Accordingly, a paper, 'Calculation Method for Hot Rolling of Steel Sheet and Strip' was prepared and published in the *Journal of the Iron and Steel Institute*, London, in February 1967. Even today, the Gupta-Ford formula features in books on applied mechanics.

Sometime in June 1964, Prof. Ford chaired a meeting at the Institution of Metals at Harrow Gate. The subject was Metals versus Plastic. He requested me to accompany him. He had so many doctoral and post-doctoral students to choose from that it surprised me when he asked me to come along. The upshot of the meeting was that a lot of metal parts in manufacturing would be replaced with composite plastic ones in the near future.

I found in Prof. Ford a truly great teacher, a brilliant scientist, an excellent practical engineer and a very good human being. He took immense care to nurture his students. Our friendship continued well beyond our days at Imperial College. It is with a sense of deep pride and privilege that I look upon my association of over 35 years with late Prof. Ford.

Prof. Ford would always mention to me that one can achieve anything in the world provided one did not seek credit for the same.

Several decades later, in 1998, Prof. Ford penned me a beautiful letter that I still treasure:

> I often think of that far off day when you, Syamal, arrived in my room at Imperial and I am always glad that, despite the fact that as Head of Department I did not normally take Research Students, your story so impressed me that I made the sudden decision to make an exception! Just think how,

had I not done so, our wonderful friendship that has lasted so happily for all these years might never have happened.

I read the article in the Tata International House journal. Yours has been a career of which anyone would be proud and forgive me if I bask a little in your sunshine as having had a small part in it, without detracting anything from your own achievements.

Now you start on a new activity for Tata on a wider front and I know you have much to give in this.

On the successful completion of the course in 1965, I continued with my research work in British Steel to study the continuous fully automated hot and cold strip mills which were then new in Europe. However, TISCO called me back as my study leave was over.

Back to TISCO

I was ready to be with the steel company that had sponsored my study at Imperial College and also the trip for my research work at British Steel. In those days, not many companies paid this kind of attention to career development, but then, generosity of many kinds has always been an integral part of the Tata culture. Needless to say, I shall never forget the help and assistance extended by TISCO and all my seniors as well as my colleagues at such a formative stage of my life; that too, when I had served the company for only seven years.

The pressure from TISCO Administration was now mounting for my return to Jamshedpur and I realized that I could not delay things any further. With a heavy heart, I informed Prof. Ford that I will not be able to pursue further studies as my company wanted me to return to India immediately.

Little did I know then that my deep connection with Prof. Ford and my relationship with Imperial College would continue to grow wider and stronger over the coming decades. I would frequently meet Prof. Ford and Sir Eric Ash, rector of the Imperial College, when on visits to the UK, or whenever they visited India through the British Council or on behalf of Imperial College. Taking advantage of their visits, we would arrange for them to address selected groups from Tata Exports, Tata Consulting Engineers, Tata Projects and other Tata companies, to exchange notes on the latest developments and practices in the respective fields. This way, our engineers would get an opportunity to interact with these visiting luminaries from Imperial College, which was always a rewarding experience.

Sir Eric Ash is a brilliant scientist, engineer, researcher and a great teacher. He contributed significantly in building the institution. He also put a lot of effort in promoting the Imperial College globally. He and his wife built and maintained the alumni relationship to new heights and our good personal relationship continues to this day.

In 1993, I was appointed a visiting professor in Imperial College's Mechanical Engineering Department, where my friend, Colin Besant was a full-fledged professor. That same year, Imperial College awarded me with their prestigious Fellowship, the highest award bestowed by the college. I received the Fellowship at a glittering Commemoration Day ceremony held at the Royal Albert Hall, London. The award citation speech by the Chairman read:

Sharp ears among you may already have noted the name Gupta in the roll call of RCS graduates this afternoon, and it is a very happy coincidence that our next Fellow is here not only to be presented to you, Chairman, but also as a parent of a fresh graduate.

It testifies to happy memories of his own time at IC that Syamal Gupta sent his own daughter here to study physics. I hope it also testifies to the belief of one of India's most outstanding examples of combined engineering and business abilities that fundamental science has an important role in our changing world.

Mr Gupta exemplifies many of the Imperial College traditions of which we are most proud: an open door to able young students from the whole world but especially from the Commonwealth, a close coupling between the research in our engineering departments and the needs of industry, and our recognition that many of our very best overseas students will move on from the research laboratory and the drawing office to the boardrooms of the companies that build up the economic strength of their countries.

Mr Gupta came to us as a graduate student of Sir Hugh Ford, in Mechanical Engineering, already crowned with laurels from his superiors in the Tata Iron and Steel Company for his contributions to the operation of their mill at Jamshedpur, and he returned there after his time with us, to begin the steady climb which brought him to his present eminence as Managing Director and Vice-Chairman of the Tata Exports Ltd. The world outside India did not forget him and he is not only a Fellow of the City & Guilds of London Institute, but also only the second Indian to be elected a Foreign Member of the Royal Academy of Engineering.

Nor did he forget us, for although the festival of Ganesh has recently passed, if the elephant never forgets, Syamal Gupta shares that feature with the elephant-headed God. He has kept in touch with the College through the years especially through Sir Hugh Ford and more recently Sir Eric Ash. As someone who was in the Physics Department when he was at IC, I am especially pleased that one of his strongest memories is of encouragement by the kind gentleman he met in the Physics Common Room whom he afterwards learnt to be our Nobel Laureate, P.M.S. Blackett.

I am sure there are young engineers in India now who will in years to come recall the encouragement of one we welcome back to IC as one of our Fellows—Mr Syamal Gupta.

To bring together the Imperial College Alumni members in India, we even formed the Imperial College India Foundation in December 2007, of which I was the chairman for some years.

With a heavy heart, I bid goodbye to London. I was sad to leave behind my professors and university colleagues, my brother and all his friends, who had been most helpful through my days of struggle. I thus boarded the Air India flight for home with mixed feelings. By the time the Boeing 707 touched Delhi, I was on a different mental plane. Sleep had eluded me. On to Calcutta, my thoughts flew faster than the aircraft. Full of plans to put my learning into practice, I was also eager to see my family, my wife and above all, to hold my little daughter, my first-born, in my arms for the first time. I was ready for Jamshedpur.

Chapter 3

HOME AGAIN

Jamshedpur's industrial history is entwined with the history of the House of Tatas, which has played a pivotal role in India's industrialization in the modern world.

In the early 1900s, when Jamsetji Tata set out to build a steel mill in British-ruled India, there were no existing steel mills or technical know-how in the country and his project would need to identify technology from the West. Jamsetji travelled to the UK seeking technical information and permissions for setting up a steel plant in India. He further visited the US in 1903 and identified reputed technologists and geologists, who soon came to India to assist in setting up a steel mill. To me, this epic initial effort of Jamsetji was a huge nationalistic endeavour to create wealth for his country and give his people economic freedom.

Prof. P.N. Bose, a renowned Indian geologist, had earlier mapped several areas of our country for sources of iron ore, petroleum and coal. He had discovered rich iron ore deposits on the Gorumahisani Hills in Mayurbhanj State (now in Odisha), then ruled by a maharajah during the British period. Prof. Bose wrote a letter to Jamsetji Tata in February 1904 informing him about the iron ore deposits in this region and conveying the intention of the maharaja to utilize the iron ore mines for processing metals.

Shortly, however, Jamsetji passed away in Bad Nauheim, Germany, and his son, Sir Dorabji Tata, took on the task of realizing his father's ambitious project and dream. Sir Dorabji Tata and his team identified Sakchi village in present day Jamshedpur, which was near the meeting point of two rivers, Kharkai and Subernarekha, as a possible site for setting up the steel plant, with assured supply of raw material from the iron ore mines of Gorumahisani and adjoining coal fields.

Dorabji Tata tried hard to raise funds for this ambitious iron and steel mill project. He went to London in 1907 to raise finances, but came back empty handed and disappointed when British bankers refused to support him. He did not give up and decided to raise money from fellow Indians and thus came about the first offering of public shares in India. The Indian population generously supported the project. TISCO was registered on 27 August 1907 with an initial capital of ₹2 crore. In 1911, TISCO Township, the first planned modern city of India was ready. In February 1912, the first ingot of steel rolled out of the Steel Works.

Soon after the end of the First World War, on his visit to Sakchi, Lord Chelmsford, as the viceroy of India, renamed the township Jamshedpur in honour of Jamsetji Tata. The name of the railway station was also changed thereafter from Kalimati to Tatanagar. Jamshedpur was not only an industrial centre at that time, but a destination for many involved in India's struggle for Independence. Mahatma Gandhi, Dr Rajendra Prasad, Jawaharlal Nehru and Subhas Chandra Bose were among the leaders who visited the steel city. At a difficult time in 1928, when a disruptive union declared a lock-out, Subhas Chandra Bose assumed the president's post of Jamshedpur Labour Association and sought to mediate a settlement.

Almost the entire city and its infrastructure is managed by TISCO, ranging from schools, good hospitals and free medical assistance in a number of clinics set up in the township, to subsidized housing, playgrounds and parks, good paved roads, good dairy and poultry products, and many other such facilities. When I landed in Jamshedpur, I found the city to be clean and well-maintained, with less than a hundred thousand people. There were no power cuts, we had ample water, and good club houses to relax and indulge in recreational activities.

In Jamshedpur, I reported to the chief engineer to re-join TISCO at my old grade and salary. Soon, I was promoted to design engineer-in-charge of a section in the Design Department. Around this time, in 1964–65, CEDD was re-organized. The Engineering & Development Department was created within CEDD to evaluate new technology and processes; suggest projects for diversification; facilitate import substitution and carry out technology evaluations. I was appointed as research engineer in this new department in April 1965.

Within a few months of my appointment, the chief development engineer left the company and I was asked to manage the department, as a replacement was yet to be found. In such a scenario, giving first preference to a suitable departmental candidate was the normal practice at TISCO. Accordingly, the department recommended me for the position as I had the requisite qualifications and experience. However, the Personnel Department had already planned to advertise the position in India and the UK to select the right candidate. I too applied and appeared before the interview board in November 1967. I was finally selected and appointed as chief development engineer in February 1968.

Around this time, Mahalingam introduced me to Ratan Tata. Ratan had returned from the US and had already spent a couple of years in TELCO and TISCO. He was then assigned to CEDD and later appointed technical assistant to S.K. Nanavati, the director-in-charge at TISCO. Ratan is a modest and intelligent person with no airs about him and proactive in everything he does. He speaks freely with everyone and tries to do on his own whatever job was entrusted to him. We worked closely with Ratan in the Engineering Department. We discussed and tried to evaluate some of the new technologies, which were coming up, and the economic milieu.

Growth Shop

In the mid-1960s, with foreign exchange being scarce, the Indian government had severely restricted the import of capital goods, spare parts and raw materials as also foreign investments and overseas travels. This made import of capital equipment difficult and prices were soaring. Therefore, as a step towards self-reliance, Moolgaokar suggested setting up a 'Growth Shop' at TISCO, in line with the Growth Shop in TELCO. This unit was ideated to be capable of designing and manufacturing critical capital goods, spares and equipment for TISCO as needed, for its growth and maintenance. The Growth Shop created capacity and saved money as we manufactured locally rather than import the machinery. Thus, despite government restrictions, there were no business losses.

As vice chairman of TISCO and Tata Motors, Moolgaokar was trying to bring these two companies together in many ways. Although both companies had their own business plans, offered different products and services and their individual paths took them on different journeys, Moolgaokar arranged for the people from TISCO and TELCO to meet and work together. The intention was to utilize common facilities and special capabilities available in these companies in terms of research and manufacturing which would be of mutual interest.

As Moolgaokar said, 'A company has to constantly grow younger. It has to grow not just in size, but in productivity and technology as well. You have got to give the technicians the fun and excitement of growth. In a developing country, if you are importing a crane, it is no challenge; but if you make one, you give your technicians fresh skills. It is part of a manager's duty to give that challenge to his people.'

Ratan was assigned to prepare the detailed project for setting up the Growth Shop. He worked on the Growth Shop project between 1967 and 1968. This was one of his first major projects in TISCO. While preparing the project report, Ratan meticulously studied a wide range of parts and components required for the plant and gathered information, drawings and data from the TISCO Machine Shop and TELCO Growth Shop. With all these details, Ratan was able to plan the capacity of the plant, fabrication, machining and other details. He further prepared the layout, flow of material, manpower, and manning of the plant, together with its operating cost. The final report was submitted to Nanavati in 1968, and promptly approved by the Board. TISCO Growth Shop was completed and inaugurated in 1969.

N.P. Naik, a brilliant engineer; D.P. Kharia, general manager at TISCO and Mahalingam provided guidance for the development of the project. Naik was later appointed as the divisional manager of the Growth Shop for the implementation and operation of the project. The TISCO Growth Shop turned out to be a great success. It made equipment worth millions of dollars. What started out as a move towards import substitution, grew in scale to become a large step in the right direction under Moolgaokar. The foreign exchange restrictions also sparked other innovations.

Colour Coating

The constraints on import of zinc had resulted in TISCO virtually stopping production of galvanized sheets as roofing material for consumers at large. The Engineering Development Department was exploring alternate solutions to the problem, as requested by the management.

One day, the chief engineer asked me to accompany him to meet K.H. Kutar, general manager of TISCO. Kutar requested the chief engineer to explore the possibilities of developing a pilot plant for colour coating of black sheets to evaluate the products. Colour-coated sheets are a high-value item in addition to providing enhanced life and better aesthetics. Kutar mentioned that he has seen colour-coated steel in Japan and I too had earlier recommended manufacturing of colour-coated steel in my foreign tour report.

Kutar was aware that colour coating is done only on cold rolled galvanized strips, which gives greater protection and aesthetics. We initiated experiments on small sheets with chemical cleaning and coating materials, after consultation with the experts. We already had the experience and knowledge of continuous running of colour coating lines, based on which we had developed a process flow of batch production of small sheets. Shivaji Singh and others in the department worked closely with me to implement the project. Accordingly, we prepared a layout with separate tanks for cleaning, pickling, phosphating, chromating and drying before coating the product with a roller coater. We then established a process flow for cleaning and coating. The process of identifying the right chemicals and polymers for the colour coating was a big challenge. The plant and equipment were fabricated and installed in a building opposite the R&D laboratory. Simultaneously, trial production was done when we tested the products for quality and weathering. These were conducted by Daraius Sethna, research metallurgist at Tata Steel.

Eventually, the pilot plant was commissioned and put into operation, just in time for JRD's visit. He spent a lot of time with us, looking around the plant and equipment. He took a keen interest in talking to the staff and we were amazed to see his enthusiasm in knowing more about anything new. By encouraging us to move with the times and to achieve excellence, he left us feeling impressed and awed.

Close on the heels of the chairman's visit, Mahalingam accompanied Moolgaokar to the plant. A soft-spoken individual by nature and a visionary with a meticulous eye for detail, Moolgaokar was visibly impressed with the set up. He enquired about the process, plant and equipment, resins and PVC. Moolgaokar too was happy to see the fully operational pilot plant, which was designed, fabricated and installed within a few weeks' time. Those were exciting times, as we were constantly endeavouring to do new things and explore fresh areas of technology. This project, which was set up for import substitution, was greatly appreciated and Kutar was indeed very glad.

It may not be out of place to mention here that many decades later, in 2005, Tata Steel set up a joint venture in Pune, between TISCO and Bluescope of Australia, for manufacturing colour-coated sheets and strips. They were of course utilizing cold-rolled strips with high tolerance. Ratan, as the Group's chairman, inaugurated the Bluescope Plant and on the sideline, he mentioned that while Bluescope had now started making colour-coated sheets, TISCO had already done some R&D work years back. He further added, 'Go and ask Syamal, he knows everything.' People approached me and I told them how that project had stirred great excitement those days.

There is another interesting story about Agrico—an agricultural machinery company acquired by TISCO in the 1930s. The unit was not performing well. Labour costs were high, the yield was low and the pricing uncompetitive. Ratan was given the job to analyse the key business problems and come up with a workable solution. Not only did he spend time analysing the costing of materials, the yield and the production process, he would also walk around the factory speaking with the workers, trying to understand what actually caused the problem. It was during these interactions that he stumbled across a key fact. There was a high incentive bonus on painting agricultural implements, such as the pick and the *pauras* (shovels), to prevent rusting. The normal process was to paint the surface by brush and incentives were fixed on that basis.

In order to speed up the process, the workers were putting dozens of picks and *pauras* on an iron rod and dipping the portion that needed paint in a rectangular, shallow, paint-filled pit. Naturally, this led to a huge increase in production, followed by disproportionate incentives and high costs. Ratan amicably rationalized the incentive scheme and resolved the issue.

The Engineering Development Department was an exciting place as we were always involved in studying new processes that paved the way for innovations. Other innovations like metal stitching and twisted bar were also developed by our team.

Ratan's Initiatives

When Ratan was with TISCO, Jamshedpur, he interacted with everyone around him. He would invite us to his home and we would be awestruck, looking at his room full of exciting electronic gadgets. He was passionate about music systems and would often be found setting up speakers, radios and transmitters, devoting a lot of time in trying to improve their quality and productiveness. He had an inquisitive mind and an endearing personality, always excited about exploring new ideas and learning new things. He was also a voracious reader. I had great respect for his innate drive to always learn something new, keeping abreast of technology and development and using it for the good of society.

Ratan drove an imported American car, which sometimes would not work, primarily because it was difficult to replace the imported parts with spares. One day we were leaving the office and found Ratan waiting for his car to be returned by the mechanic. He had no idea how long it would take. In those days, connectivity was not as easy as it is today (there was no telephone in the garage and of course there were no mobile phones), so there was nothing one could do to get in touch with the mechanic.

On seeing me, Ratan asked, 'My car has not come yet. May I take a ride with you?'

'Ratan, I have a scooter, not a car.' I pointed out.

'I know you have a scooter, why don't you give me a ride,' he insisted.

To my utter amazement, Ratan was asking for a ride on my scooter! I still tried to dissuade him. 'Ratan we have so many company cars; why don't you take one of them?'

But he was adamant. 'I know, but I want to take a ride with you on your scooter.'

Now, Ratan is a tall and well-built person and I was a little worried how he would ride pillion. But he did! We rode on my scooter through the streets of Jamshedpur to his Kaizer bungalow. (The bungalows were constructed to accommodate the engineering staff of Kaizer, and so the name stuck.) He said he was enjoying the ride, but also reminded me frequently to be careful lest he gets thrown off the seat. I could see people watching us in amazement and I am sure this became the talk of the town for some time. To him, it seemed like the most natural thing on earth! His simplicity, spontaneity and care for people have always amazed us.

Ratan initiated another exciting project while in Jamshedpur— that of starting a flying club. He thought a flying club would give the necessary impetus to encourage young people to fly. It is still in operation today.

Apart from his technical ability and his mission and commitment, what endeared him to everyone in Jamshedpur was his good human nature. Everybody would lovingly address him as 'Ratan—the jewel,' which aptly described him as a human being.

Becoming a Manager

The culture at TISCO was always energetic. Mr Moolgaokar created a lot of enthusiasm among the young engineers, such that we always had something different or new to look forward to. At TISCO, the top leadership was committed to continuous development and growth. The management stressed the need for the steel company to adopt newer technologies, new product development and practices.

I recall going into meetings where JRD and Moolgaokar would be sitting along with Nanavati and other top bosses, whom we otherwise never ever got a chance to see. We were among the younger lot then, still in our 30s and 40s. Yet at the meetings, the top leadership would encourage us to think about the future technology of steel, new products, possibilities of diversification and improvement in company performance.

Just think about it. We hear about management development programmes today, but 50 years ago, we saw the top brass of TISCO—the chairman, vice chairman, managing director, all interacting with us youngsters on a one-to-one basis, encouraging us to participate and come up with innovative ideas and solutions.

Product Diversifications

Svenska Kullagerfabriken (SKF), a world leader in the manufacture of ball and roller bearings, had a modern manufacturing setup in Pune. They were major OEM suppliers of these products to TELCO and to other industries in the country. They imported raw materials, rings and tubes from their parent organization located in Gothenburg, Sweden. Due to the import restrictions at that time, they had to apply to the government of India for an import licence for semi-finished raw materials. They were subsequently told by the government to develop indigenous sources as import substitution.

SKF requested Moolgaokar to help them develop suitable manufacturers in India for quality rolled rings, a raw material for the ball bearing industry. However, there was no indigenous manufacturing plant in the country for this product. Moolgaokar thus felt it would be a good idea for TISCO to explore the possibilities of entering this business, more so as it was a semi-finished product and outside the JPC product pricing. (JPC is the erstwhile Joint Plant Committee constituted in 1964 by the government of India for formulating guidelines for production, allocation, pricing and distribution of iron and steel materials). The job of preparing a detailed project report to establish the viability of the project was entrusted to us in the CEDD Engineering Department.

After a lot of study and discussions, it was decided that we should have a medium-frequency induction furnace—an electric heating furnace to provide uniform heat to the SAE 52100 bars and avoid scaling. The entire process was new and interesting for us. However, even though SKF had undertaken to buy our entire production, to be on the safe side, we also visited other ball and roller bearing manufacturers in India and SKF in Pune.

The project called for an investment of ₹3–4 crore. The Project Report was prepared and submitted to the managing director. It was then forwarded to Moolgaokar at the Head Office in Bombay (now Mumbai) for his perusal. Moolgaokar then visited Jamshedpur and I got a call to meet him at the Director's Bungalow. While I was enthused, I was also tense to meet the Vice Chairman alone for the first time.

When I entered the Director's Bungalow, I noticed him sitting there, calm and quiet. We exchanged pleasantries and then he said he had gone through the report and found the project interesting. He touched upon the details of the plant, equipment and raw material, and finally asked whether any technical collaboration was necessary. I expressed my opinion, assuring him that we did not need any technical collaboration. However, we may only need to import the first set of tools, after which we would be able to design the tools ourselves—of that we were confident.

Moolgaokar made his decision and informed me that TISCO would be approving the project, and asked me to develop the project, prepare the layout of the plant, finalize the specification of equipment, and build my own organization. 'It will be an independent division within TISCO. Unlike other departments here, the division will be responsible for its execution, operation and functioning as a viable unit,' he instructed. I could barely realize what was happening. In our short meeting together, the decision of a few crore rupees, which was big money in those days, had been finalized!

Circulars were issued at once and I was appointed as manager of the Ring Rolling Mill in 1970. The next day, I moved from the comforts of my Engineering Office to a make-shift site office at Adityapur, a suburb of Jamshedpur, which was in stark contrast to the city. We would need to build everything. We started the work and the mill was commissioned in March 1971. My role was to develop the project, implement it, start production and market the rolled ring products to ball bearing companies in India as well as overseas. In January 1972, I was appointed the divisional manager.

This was a huge life-changing move for me as I had to shift from design, project planning and development to take charge of a newly created division, reporting directly to the managing director. My journey from being an engineer to becoming a manager had begun. I hardly realized its significance at that time.

Challenges of a New Assignment

The big day arrived when we first offered our rolled ring products to SKF. They pointed out that they would prefer to import these products as our quality did not match their expectations. I went to their headquarters in Stockholm and explained to them that the quality of our products matched their specifications. But SKF India did not relent and they continued to import their products from Sweden and told us that our products were being tested for quality.

Having spent months setting up this unit, I was not ready to give up just yet. I was personally committed to prove the quality of the products and the viability of the project. Driven by the desire to keep the plant fully loaded with or without SKF, the original people who wanted us to make the roll rings, I started exploring the overseas market. I committed to myself that whatever the situation, the products had to be viable for the international market. I was driven by the conviction that if we were accepted by the global market, breaking through the local market would then be easy. I kept the dialogue with SKF open and tried to export some products to other overseas companies, though without much success. I was disappointed, but not defeated.

We then went about marketing our products in India. There were not many ball bearing companies in India other than SKF, but there were some who were new in the field including Antifriction Bearing Company (ABC), Pune; Sri Ram Bearings Ltd, Ranchi; and Indo-Nippon Precision Bearing Co. I met all of them and explained to them the superior quality and advantages of our roll-ring products for ball and roller bearings. Rolled products were actually better than tubes because of the grain structure and other technical advantages. There would be better yield, less wastage, more uniformity of crystal structure, etc.

ABC Bearings showed some interest in using our roll-ring products. They were new and trying to establish themselves in the ball bearing industry and hence were interested in looking at rolled-rings as an alternative to tubes. I finally met M.I. Patel, chairman of ABC Bearings and an open-minded person. Finally, ABC Bearings decided to switch to rolled rings in a big way. This was a great success and our first product was supplied to them. I was happy and thankful to Patel for encouraging us to set up this industry for rolled rings that are key in several mechanical applications.

We started receiving more orders and soon the plant was loaded. We were making quality products and were even thinking of expansion, when SKF finally came back to us to place its order. The plant was running smoothly and with a full order book.

On 2 March 1971, a high-level team including the top brass of TISCO led by JRD, Moolgaokar and Nanavati visited the Ring Rolling Plant. All of us were on tenterhooks. We knew of JRD and Moolgaokar's penchant for quality and their uncompromising standards on industrial hygiene and employee welfare. So, it was a great relief when this high-level visit concluded with the distinguished team members expressing their satisfaction at the way the project was shaping up. JRD and the team complimented us for putting up such a great plant. Though it was a small mill compared to TISCO, it was one of our first successful attempts to diversify and to manufacture products out of the JPC price-controlled list.

The success of the ring rolling mill project was possible because of the tremendous support from the managing director, the chief engineer and others in Jamshedpur. It was also due, in a big way, to Moolgaokar's continuous encouragement, his unwavering faith in people, and his unique method of creating an entrepreneurial spirit; of confidence building and encouraging young minds to think big. I recall his advice when he once wrote to me:

> There is a belief in our country that our culture and our Indian character cannot allow our people to attain consistently high standards, that shoddiness and carelessness are our God-given, unalterable way of life. But if, with faith in them, you ask our men for their best, they rise to your belief and in their worth to create a momentum towards improvement. Often, I have seen men who are considered ordinary, rise to extraordinary heights. Do not accept second-rate work; expect the best, ask for it, pursue it relentlessly and you will get it.

These deep words of advice stood me in good stead even in the later years at Tata. When faced with the most daunting situations, I drew upon the innate wisdom of these words which has shown me the direction, time and again.

Drive for Globalization

By this time, Tatas were also looking overseas for opportunities. The industry in India was undergoing trying times. We were predominantly an agricultural economy, dependent on and prone to the vagaries of nature. India had adopted a socialistic pattern of development and was working hard to rebuild itself. However, excessive government controls or the License Raj, as it was referred to, stifled both business and industry, as red tape and bureaucracy-ruled.

In the midst of this stifling environment, the Tatas stood tall and refused to believe that this was the end of the road. They constantly looked upon challenges as opportunities and their pioneering zeal burns bright to this day. The Tatas were convinced that if they had to augment their contribution towards India's development, their vision now needed to move beyond national boundaries.

This desire was actually triggered in September 1966, when TISCO was invited by the government of Iran to explore the possibility of setting up a narrow strip and tube mill in Iran. This was possibly one of our first overseas projects. The Industrial and Mining Development Bank of Iran wanted to establish facilities at Ahwaz, Iran, for the manufacture of skelp and tubes. The bank was interested in Tatas' participation in the project both from the development as well as operational side, along with the consulting engineering firm, F.W. Eske of London.

This project was entrusted to CEDD to study and to prepare a detailed project report. Ratan took the lead in the project. We worked night and day alongside Ratan to prepare a detailed project report that included the layout information, required plant and machinery, power, water and financials. The report was prepared and handed over to Nanavati literally in the nick of time, with the aircraft waiting to take off for Iran. One can imagine the enthusiasm, the excitement and the euphoria. The Tatas were going to quote for a prestigious overseas project. This became the talk of the town.

Our happiness was, however, short-lived when we discovered much to our horror, a zero missing in our estimates—a typographical error! Ratan spoke to the senior bosses and he was able to communicate the change in the figure to Nanavati just in time. Although, we did not get the job, the learning was immense. The desire to look beyond the borders of India had just been ignited.

The Tata Group continuously looked for globalization for its development and growth. At that point, two Tata companies— Tata Limited, London, and Tata Incorporated, USA—were looking after the interests of the Tata Group from foreign shores. They were established primarily for procurement of materials for group companies in India and also to explore business opportunities, without which it was difficult for those companies to survive, let alone thrive. Their sole source of income was the commission they earned for procuring goods.

Sometime in the late 1960s, Tata Zug was formed in Zurich. The objective of this company was to explore the possibilities of developing new business in Europe and elsewhere, and it was headed by Farrokh Kavarana, a brilliant chartered accountant from London with an MBA degree from Wharton. He took over the responsibility of Tata Zug and Tata AG to explore possibilities of collaboration and also investment in business opportunities in Europe. Kavarana, at that time, was possibly the youngest director on the Board of Tata Industries.

At the same time, around November 1969, Tata Dalgety, headed by Ratan Tata, was formed in Australia. This joint venture between Dalgety and Tatas was intended to explore the possibilities of business in Australia and to advance cooperation between the two countries.

JRD, Moolgaokar and Dr Freddie Mehta, chief economic advisor to Tatas, visited Australia. They met Ratan and Dalgety executives and also had meetings with government officials. Alongside these meetings, Dr Mehta briefed JRD and Moolgaokar about the phenomenal progress made in Singapore under the stewardship of Lee Kuan Yew. It was decided that on their return from Australia, they would break journey at Singapore, which till today continues to be a natural transit point between the two countries. Dr Mehta arranged a meeting with the finance minister of Singapore, Dr Goh Keng Swee, who had not only been Dr Mehta's senior at the London School of Economics, but the two knew each other quite well.

All Eyes on Singapore

History reveals that most countries under foreign domination have had to struggle to gain their Independence. Singapore's history, however, is different. Independence was thrust upon it and it was forced, as it were, to accept Independence. This tiny 'fishing village' woke up to face the stark reality of having virtually nothing but unemployment, poor living conditions and not one industry worth a mention. To add to this, there was the mafia, mistrust and disturbances strewn all over.

In the midst of this chaotic situation, a towering figure, Cambridge-educated lawyer, Lee Kuan Yew (LKY) rose to take charge and to rewrite the history of the nation in a manner no one had done in the past. But those were trying times. A nation had to be built from scratch. LKY got together a team of individuals who matched his dedication to the task at hand. Together, they set out their priorities—housing and health for all, education, infrastructure and skill development, and industrialization to be methodically encouraged.

While the ideologies pursued by India and Singapore then, were different, both countries were working hard at creating a better future for their people. India had adopted a socialistic pattern of development with heavy focus on equitable distribution of wealth and all-round development. Though exports were encouraged, India did not have too many industrial products to export. Besides, technology and innovation were only permitted to the extent that they substituted imports, which were severely restricted. Money was scarce.

An interesting story is often recounted when talking about the historic meeting that took place in Singapore on 26 April 1970, of the three gentlemen from India—JRD, Moolgaokar and Dr Mehta with Dr Goh Keng Swee and Dr Hon Sui Sen, the then chairman of Singapore's Economic Development Board (EDB).

Dr Goh said that foreign direct investment was most welcome and that there were no controls on repatriation of profits. He also explained the government's desire to get into higher value engineering industry, stating that precision industry was very much on the list. The Singapore government's strategy was clear. It wanted to give all the basic needs to industry so that it could work peacefully in Singapore and earn enough money. Dr Goh spoke about factors like free market economy in Singapore and flexible rules and regulations. The only criterion that Singapore was emphatic about was that business should be profitable.

Dr Goh told JRD that he wanted the Tatas to make as much money as possible out of their venture in Singapore. JRD was wondering if he had heard him right. Dr Goh explained that this was actually a win-win strategy for all. The greater the profits that the Tatas would make, the greater the share would be of the Singapore government and the higher the bonuses that would be paid to the workers. The three Tata stalwarts were impressed with the deliberations and they decided to have a serious look at Singapore and South-East Asia.

On their return to India, a high-level team was set up at the Head Office with Dr Mehta as co-ordinator to lead the group activities of our foreign operations. Other members of this team were Arun Maira, deputy general manager at TELCO and Abinava Qazi, development engineer. It was further decided to send a three-member team for about 10 days to Singapore and South-East Asia, under B. Nehru, managing director, Tata Exports. M.N. Bagai, senior divisional manager at TELCO, and I were the other two members.

I was called to the Head Office and met Dr Mehta who briefed me about their visit to Singapore and discussed the country's economy and business. I also had a meeting with Moolgaokar who was excited about Singapore and briefed me about the possibilities. Our three-member team visited Malaysia, Indonesia, Thailand and Singapore in July 1970.

On our return, I reported:

> Singapore's investment climate is excellent. Substantial incentives are offered by the government in terms of tax holidays, liberal licensing policy and financial assistance. Open door policy for foreign investment and free repatriation of profits have already attracted large foreign investments to the Island.

The proposition was interesting and quite contrary to the prevailing scenario in India those days.

Deliberations and Coming on Board

Singapore was eager to have the Tatas participate in their development programme. To this end they offered many attractive incentives including a pioneering status. In the meantime, multinationals like General Electrics (GE), Philips and Siemens were already in Singapore, but more as assembly units. The Singapore government wanted these industries to add value. However, in order to go up the value chain, the MNCs needed precision components and support services of tool rooms. In view of this requirement, the Singapore government and EDB held discussions with Tatas, Philips and Siemens to consider putting up a high-precision industry to support their manufacturing.

For the Tatas, this appeared to be a good opportunity—to enter Singapore as an industrial group, and participate in its development programme, within the overall objective. Moolgaokar was of the firm belief that through Singapore, the Tata Group would succeed in reaching out to the rest of the world in industries not known to India in those days. It would give Tatas unparalleled access to companies like GE, Philips, Siemens and semi-conductor and computer peripheral industries.

The Tatas needed this base outside Indian shores to have access to world-class technology and global markets and in the process take India to greater heights. Moolgaokar decided to forge ahead with the idea and initiated the process. The company was going to be named Tata Precision Industries Pte Ltd. This was going to be the first major industry set up abroad by the Tatas.

All energies were now directed towards making TPI a reality in the shortest time possible. The TPI team in the Head Office at Mumbai, under the leadership of Dr Mehta, initiated action towards the project. Maira and Qazi of TELCO were part of the team. Several senior managers in TELCO also visited Singapore a number of times to meet potential customers and prepared a market survey report. Ramanathan, a TELCO manager, visited Singapore to meet consultants, contractors and others to estimate the cost of putting up the plant.

TELCO Pune, was preparing a detailed project report (DPR), including the list of machine tools. Moolgaokar was clear that he wanted only the very best machinery for TPI and he personally selected all the machine tools and evaluated all the plant and equipment requirements. Finally, a DPR showing tentative layout of the plant and equipment, size of the building, power requirements, manpower planning and capital costs was put together that was finally approved by Moolgaokar. TPI was turning out a capital-intensive project and as the report indicated, it would take about five years for TPI to become profitable.

The DPR was submitted to EDB, and other potential partners and banks. To ease the pressure, EDB offered to make TPI's pioneer status as an umbrella, so that the tax-free period would be extended to all activities that TPI undertook. Sime Darby, a

Malaysian trading conglomerate had already expressed interest in taking up a minority shareholding in TPI. Two banks—Citibank, with whom Tata International already had a connection, and the Development Bank of Singapore (DBS)—were also consulted. The response of DBS was the most significant, and over a period of time, it proved to be a source of great strength to us. S. Dhanabalan, the vice chairman of DBS (who was also later inducted into the Singapore government as foreign minister) was quite impressed. He could see that TPI was going to be much more than a Tata venture outside India. It was to be the bridge that would bring the two countries together.

In the meantime, Dr Goh visited TELCO Plant in Pune as did executives of EDB and others from Singapore to get first-hand knowledge about the company's technical operations and its training skills. Everyone—Singapore's finance minister and EDB executives—was greatly impressed with the plant and its training facilities.

From a long-term perspective, it was felt that a precision engineering complex must be eventually supported by a training school to offer skilled toolmakers. The training school would provide the 'skills' to the Tool-Room Plant, which in turn would become the nucleus of an entire precision-engineering complex. EDB and Tatas would jointly set up a training school for grooming technicians in precision engineering.

Ng Pock Too, a young and dynamic officer at EDB, was responsible for developing and finalizing the Tata project. Singapore's warm welcome, determination, persistence and willingness to go the extra mile finally prevailed and the decision was made—Tatas would be happy to partner with Singapore.

The Chosen One

The defining moment finally unfolded in June 1971 when the

TPI project was approved by the Singapore government. By this time, Dr Goh had handed over the reins of the Finance Ministry to Dr Hon Sui Sen. Dr Mehta, N.R. Mody, A.B. Billimoria, S.R. Vakil and A.N. Maira from Tata visited Singapore and held several meetings with the concerned authorities and finally with the finance minister, Dr Sui Sen and Dr Tang, chairman of EDB. Maira played an important role in liaising between the Singapore government and Tatas in finalizing the joint venture.

The next question was who would lead this venture? The Group's top directors comprising of JRD, Moolgaokar and Mehta scanned all the probable candidates and finally decided upon my name for the new venture. In March 1971, I was told that my next assignment would require me to be in Singapore. Partnering the TPI business were Tata International AG; Sime Darby Holdings; DBS and TELCO. Unfortunately, India's tight foreign exchange regulations at the time precluded TELCO from making a direct financial contribution to TPI. The total authorized capital of the company was to be S$5 (Singapore $5) million. The borrowing would be another S$5 million, with Citibank providing S$300,000 and the balance coming from DBS.

The first four directors of the company were Naval Mody of Tata Inc. as chairman, Dr Freddie A. Mehta of Tata Sons, Nick Young of Sime Darby and Dhanabalan of DBS. The Board appointed Ramaswamy and me as alternate directors, authorized to attend board meetings in the absence of overseas directors.

This was to be the first major venture of the Tatas outside India, and to have them repose their confidence in me, filled me with zeal to once again rise to the occasion.

Chapter 4

TAKING CHARGE IN SINGAPORE

Singapore is an island surrounded by the Indian Ocean and two countries: Indonesia on one side and Malaysia on the other. When I landed in Singapore in 1972, the country had no raw materials and even drinking water had to be imported. There was no major infrastructure, the population was young and foreign exchange was restricted. Yet, the stagnating economy of the 1960s that suffered chronic labour problems, had transformed into a throbbing one, resulting in an affluent society.

With a dynamic and far-sighted policy of rapid industrialization, the Singapore government was able to solve its problem of unemployment, resulting in stability. Much of this is attributed to LKY and his team's plan to develop and transform Singapore from a third-world country to a first-world nation within a definite span of time.

Singapore's leadership was focused on nation-building and aggressively promoted export-oriented, labour-intensive industrialization via an incentive programme geared to attract foreign investment. The EDB, established in 1961, was responsible for promoting Singapore as a place of business in order to attract foreign capital. EDB officers went around the US and other countries in western Europe, promoting Singapore as the right place to build competitive manufacturing bases for big corporations. Singapore was being projected as a politically stable country with a productive workforce that communicated in English with fair ease.

In order to attract the MNCs, the EDB provided a manufacturing base in Singapore by developing Jurong Industrial Town. Jurong, though marshy and reclaimed from the sea, was earmarked for development into an industrial zone. It offered ready-to-move-in factories. EDB was also empowered to offer pioneer status to suitable foreign corporations with tax benefits up to a period of five years. Most foreign investors found that their production costs dropped significantly and soon many foreign corporations thronged to Singapore due to these inviting factors.

By 1972, one-quarter of Singapore's manufacturing firms was either foreign-owned, or a joint venture, and both the US and Japan were major investors. As a result of Singapore's steady political climate, favourable investment conditions and the rapid expansion of the world economy between 1965 and 1973, the country's Gross Domestic Product (GDP) experienced a steady annual double-digit growth.

With the government providing subsidized housing, education, health services and public transportation, new jobs were generated in the public sector. The Central Provident Fund, the country's comprehensive social security scheme, sustained by compulsory contributions from both the employer and employee, provided the necessary capital for government projects and financial security for the country's workforce in their old age.

This was the Singapore I stepped into with the intent of making a success of the new venture and living up to the expectations of the Group. I took charge as general manager, TPI, on 1 April 1972.

Initially, I shuttled back and forth between Singapore and Mumbai to take the project further, but I finally shifted to Singapore with my family in August 1972. Through the good offices of Young, the British director with Sime Darby, we were able to approach the Singapore government for a residential property for me and my family. It was a two-bedroom, one-storeyed bungalow, located in the heart of the city, in Goodwood Hill, that was occupied earlier by Sime Darby. My wife and children too were happy to be in Singapore and our youngest daughter was born there. For my children, Singapore had quite a few good schools that were started during the colonial days, under the British.

In 1972, when we landed in Singapore, it appeared more like a small Indian town with its narrow roads, old buildings and small corner shops. You could see a lot of Indians in dhotis selling foreign exchange in the markets. There was no current account convertibility and foreign exchange was restricted. In those days, one Singapore dollar used to be equivalent to 2.5 Indian rupees. The country had a diverse population comprising Chinese, Malay, Indian and Europeans. The people were friendly and my family and I soon developed many connections and friendships with the local people that have sustained through the years.

Setting Up a World-Class Facility

We initially set up an office in just two rooms of the centrally located Imperial Hotel. The project report and the financing were well prepared for business. My immediate tasks on hand therefore were to prepare a Plan of Action based on the DPR, establish its viability, identify our market segments and the correct products, identify the right technology while staying abreast of new developments and build the organization by acquiring the right manpower with requisite skills, targeting customers and developing relationships, gathering market intelligence and being profitable.

Having secured a pioneering status for TPI from the Singapore government, we had to execute the project, get into the market and be viable. The project implementation had to happen on schedule. We had regular meetings with EDB, most of them with Ng Pock Too. EDB allotted seven acres of land in Jurong to us. However, the construction of the TPI building was challenging and proved expensive due to the fact that Jurong Industrial Estate was built on filled up marshy land.

The creation of a business district at this location was the idea of Dr Goh Keng Swee, the then finance minister of Singapore. However, until 1965, Jurong had made little progress and cynics mocked the venture, calling it 'Goh's Folly', but after Singapore's Independence, Jurong took off, attracting a flood of investments and creating many jobs, and it was not long before it became 'Goh's Glory'. Jurong was 20 km away from the city and the land was reclaimed from the sea and transformed to become the spotlight of Singapore's industrialization. Through Dr Goh's efforts, 15,000 acres of swamp in Jurong was turned into a modern industrial park. The vast land available on an immediate basis made it an ideal site—one that was close to Singapore's Keppel Harbour, relatively flat and had a low population density. Furthermore, Jurong's coastline provided a natural deep harbour which made it ideal for Jurong Port to be set up in addition to the Keppel Harbour in the south of Singapore.

Despite the challenges of construction, Moolgaokar was happy that the best architectural materials were available in Singapore, which could be used to create a model factory comparable to the best in Germany or Switzerland. Alongside the building construction work, orders for all machinery had been placed with various Swiss and German companies through Tata Ltd, London. Many of the machines had a long lead time, but we tried to match the delivery of equipment to the completion of the building. When it came to the selection of machinery for the project, we built a state-of-the-art facility with nothing less than the very best machinery. Moolgaokar too had recommended Swiss and German machinery, which were absolutely the finest.

Upon completion of the building construction, in early 1973, the first machine was installed and within three months, all the key machines had been installed. We moved into our beautifully laid out building at 1, Liu Fang Road, Jurong, along with a team of highly skilled technicians and operators from India.

On 30 April 1973, in an internal memo to Moolgaokar, I was able to report:

> Started operating the machine tools on a trial basis, thereby fulfilling our commitments to the Singapore Government. Four Machine Tools installed and Public Utilities Board did a fine job in effecting power supply on 30 April enabling us to beat the deadline.

He immediately responded with a message to the TPI team:

Congratulations for fulfilling your commitment to the Singapore Government and for doing a fine job within the stipulated time. We were determined to keep the commitment Moolgaokar had made to the Singapore government, and yet not lose. Earlier, he had clearly expressed in a meeting with Dr Mehta and Qazi that we were committed to set up the high precision tool room in Singapore, but we should also ensure that we did not stand to lose in the bargain. To this end, Moolgaokar had requested S.Y. Jakatdar, executive director, TELCO Pune, to look into the TPI structure and see how it could be made profitable.

Jakatdar had made a series of positive suggestions to bring down costs as included in the DPR. He felt that the production costs were inflated because all machinery was being manned by highly experienced toolmakers. What the company needed was a mix of highly experienced and less experienced operators including some apprentices.

Moolgaokar's vision of building Singapore as the Tatas' window to the world was gradually taking shape. We were starting from a point of disadvantage, as we did not have the requisite skills and know-how to serve the semi-conductor industry. However, we took it upon ourselves to build capabilities that would meet international standards in precision engineering, catering to semi-conductor, computer peripheral and other related industries. This was also to be the base for the Tatas to gain exposure and expertise in marketing, technology and new product development.

Building and Training a New Team

In the early days of TPI, we operated under some challenging conditions. TPI was to service high-precision press tools and plastic moulds required for the electronic and semi-conductor industries, but this was new to us. In our core technical team we had highly qualified and experienced engineers like T.N Srinivasan, Bhanot, Bhaskar and Ms Lee. The team, along with others, were able to acquire knowledge and develop expertise so that we could enter the market.

However, Moolgaokar did not see our lack of specific know-how as a major impediment. He visualized the Singapore venture as an opportunity for us to enhance our knowledge in new materials, new equipment, new products and technology, globally. He emphasized that one must enhance one's learning to the extent of being a leader in that field. 'If the job we do is better than the best, then we go in for higher and higher skills and then there is no competition. If we keep doing it better every day, then we are right on top of the ladder,' he said.

The workforce we got from India was composed of skilled

technicians on a work permit basis. They had not taken up permanent residence. Therefore, when Singapore experienced a slight recession, some of the Indian technicians feared the loss of long-term job security and left the organization, preferring to move to Australia, Canada and other places. This proved to be one of our major challenges. Most of the Indians we recruited were from outside the Tata Group and, therefore, we had no hold on them. Besides, we had developed our own system of operations that integrated the established practice of experienced technicians that worked well for business. Thus, another difficulty we faced was to get the workforce from India to integrate with the local people due to differences in work culture.

Nelly Ng was the first Singaporean to join us as a secretary. Joyce Ng joined us as manager of personnel. Her responsibility was to formalize the organization's chart with the duties and responsibilities of the managers. She played a key role in the company and gradually moved up to be vice president, Personnel and Administration. Joyce served at TPI for many years. K. Yogalingam, a chartered accountant who had gained experience in London, joined us as manager, Accounts and Finance. He set up the department with accounting procedures and financial control of the company. The Chinese workers and professionals gave TPI long years of service; many for 30 to 35 years. I found them disciplined and committed to their job.

We also motivated our people to take up continuous training. The Singapore government decided to establish a training school and offered to assist the Tatas in setting up the Tata Government Training Centre (TGTC) jointly under the auspices of the Industrial Training Board of Singapore, TELCO and EDB. To set up the programme, the Singapore government provided TGTC adequate space in one of its existing training schools at Jurong. The government was to share the running expenses with the Tatas in the proportion of 70:30 in favour of the Tatas. Later, the Singapore government decided to take over the entire expenses of running the school.

EDB had played a major role in setting up the training school. It saw the need to train workers in preparation for the anticipated needs of various industries. However, it felt that only an industry, which best understood the demands of industry, could help run the training programmes.

Under the TGTC project, which was soon established, the Tatas provided the trainers and in return were entitled to half the toolmakers who were trained. The programme that provided a training period of two years, churned out 500 trainees over a period of six years. To encourage more Singaporeans to join the training centre, the government indicated that it would prefer TGTC to accept fresh school pass-outs and would even relax the requirements of National Service, which was compulsory for all students before they joined university. The government also suggested that TGTC consider the possibility of putting in some production-type equipment at the training school, so that the trainees could work on actual tool reconditioning and simple production jobs towards the latter part of their training. TGTC was headed by F.M.A. Shaikh of TELCO, as director of the centre. He was a highly respected person and Moolgaokar had personally selected him for this prestigious job.

Bagging the First Order

Towards the second half of the 1970s, Singapore was upgrading itself. From textile, book printing and fishing industries, it was gradually moving to an assembly of TV and other electronic goods, to actually manufacture the integrated circuits (ICs) and ultimately, even design them. Over the years, Singapore moved from basic industries to hi-tech electronics, semi-conductors and aviation. What made Singapore different was that while many other governments would give incentives to attract foreign investments, the EDB of Singapore offered them services and incentives packaged together in a 'hard not to accept' manner. The EDB trained their people well, such that they would attract multinationals to Singapore. This was in keeping with the policy of LKY's government to upgrade the country to a level where people in Singaporean society would enjoy higher standards of living.

We too realized that doing business in Singapore had to have a global reach. The Singapore market was totally integrated with the global market and had no limits on imports. As a result, all of us who were trained in an import-regulated environment had to re-orient our thinking. It was tough to understand the dynamics of the market. We, who came from a protected and fenced-off economy, had much to learn while operating in Singapore. We decided to approach the head offices of semi-conductor industries to make them aware of TPI's capabilities.

However, being a start-up contract manufacturer with no product of its own, TPI found it challenging to enlist itself with major semi-conductor and telecom companies. As neither India nor the Tatas were known for any kind of track record in this industry, our job was even more challenging. Most of the large corporations like GE, Philips, Rollei and others were naturally comfortable in placing orders with vendors who had long-standing business relations with their principals. We had to work hard to open more doors and to find alternate routes to grow our business.

We identified our potential customers and most of them were US and European MNCs. We also established contact with their local subsidiaries such as GE, Siemens, Philips, National Semiconductor, Fairchild, Texas Instruments, and many others. My colleagues and I were determined to make a breakthrough in the semi-conductor industry. Our core team made regular contacts with the customers. The need of the hour was to establish credibility, capability and marketability—in that order.

While marketing to customers, we often showed them intricate machine parts and components produced by TPI. We would invite local representatives of international companies to our manufacturing facilities. This is where Moolgaokar's vision must be appreciated greatly. He would say, 'If you want to get good food then you must have a good kitchen,' and that was how TPI was built. EDB too introduced us to a number of potential customers who were coming to Singapore to set up business.

The chairman of the Thomson Group of Companies, France, once visited our plant in Singapore. He spent a couple of hours critically examining our machine tools, layout and types of jobs being executed. He was impressed with TPI's performance. Later, he also met senior government officials and paid handsome tributes to the Tatas' pioneering contribution in the establishment of a precision engineering industry in Singapore.

The chairman of EMIL Group of Companies of Australia also paid us a visit. He too was greatly impressed by the Tatas' foresight in putting up such a well-laid-out plant with the finest quality machine tools and a beautiful factory building. While leaving, he remarked, 'I thought that Taj Mahal was located in India!'

Every enterprise will always remember its first order with much nostalgia. The same is the case with the TPI team with regard to the first order placed by GE. GE's subsidiary was located close to the TPI facility at Jurong, where GE made components for their computer facilities in the US. GE engineers who visited us were impressed with our facility, in particular, the spick and span shop. The GE engineering manager wanted TPI to first prove its capability, and before placing a full tool order, GE wanted components to be made.

The TPI team was excited. This was the moment we had been waiting for—our first order! GE continued to be our main customer in the early days. We received a steady flow of orders for precision components. GE also off-loaded to us their repair jobs for moulds and press tools. Once GE was assured of our quality and our ability to deliver on time, we received our first order for a complete, new, single-cavity mould from GE.

Building a Reputation

Those were the days of technological evolution, particularly in the semi-conductor and computer peripheral industry. The semi-conductor industry was growing rapidly and it was necessary to stay in tune with new technology. Before we could finish the design for a tool for the lead frame manufacturers, they would come up with a more powerful, smaller and more efficient version. Our products and our capabilities had to be enhanced regularly as each subsequent order came with stringent quality requirements.

Most of our engineers visited the West Coast of the US—the nerve centre of the semi-conductor industry. Nearly all the high-tech industries had good engineers, with quite a few Indians among them and it was a pleasure to see what they were doing. University connections those days proved important. We visited San Jose, Santa Clara and many small towns where young engineers and scientists lived and worked. I also visited Prof. Hugh Ford at the Imperial College, London, to discuss new products and technologies.

Our core team constantly kept in touch with customers. From tools and tackles, TPI moved on to computer peripherals, then printer components. Our efforts were soon focused on being the leader in design. This was the time of great opportunities and unique challenges. As we got involved with global companies and sunrise industries, it was necessary to enhance our capabilities. For instance, we were working with manually operated machine tools. To remain competitive, we introduced CAD/CAM technology and also arranged for the more advanced CNC machines. We had top of the line machinery from Swiss, Japanese and German manufacturers such as Studer, SIP Degussa, Deckel, Argie, Chermilles and Titutoyo. In spite of financial constraints, with the approval of Moolgaokar, TPI was able to order CNC machines. Thankfully, the decision to invest in CNCs proved to be correct as these machines introduced better quality, higher productivity and timely completion.

Within two years of operations, TPI's order book carried such big names as GE, Burroughs and Rollei, besides some semi-conductor giants like Texas Instruments, National Semi-conductor and Fairchild. The order from Aldus Plastics, Australia, was perhaps the most interesting one. They had actually placed an order for a complete injection and blow-moulding die with a Japanese toolmaker. However, due to the prevailing industrial slowdown in Japan caused by the oil shortage, serious delays were expected in manufacturing the mould. We took this opportunity and offered Aldus the timeline they required and matched the Japanese price as well. The combined injection and blow moulding was a relatively new patented process and was at that time beginning to find wide application in the industry. The mould was manufactured in our shop and we met the delivery schedule too.

In December 1973, Moolgaokar wrote:

> I am glad that as a result of your efforts the order book is growing at a satisfactory rate and now it will only be a question of time before you are able to step up your production. I do hope it will not be long before you operate all your machines on a two-shift basis and a few expensive ones even on a three-shift basis.

TPI soon earned a good name for itself. Senior industry leaders from the US and other countries visited the facilities and were impressed. Siemens AG (Germany) placed a trial order for precision stamping tools with TPI, and once Siemens was in our order books, we started receiving orders from other major international companies.

Upon the successful completion of the order, Siemens took further steps to take the relationship to the next level. To establish closer collaboration for manufacturing highly specialized tools required by their Telecommunications division, the German company sent TPI a proposal that it would provide necessary technical services and transfer specialized technology or know-how that might be necessary in manufacturing their assorted tools. Siemens would also depute to Singapore a tool and die engineer, at their cost, to assist TPI wherever necessary in making the dies and tools to their specifications. They would also provide assured workload to TPI.

In response to my message informing him about the proposed tie-up with Siemens, Moolgaokar wrote:

> I think it will be an excellent idea to follow up on the Siemens
> proposal. They are a first-rate firm and we will stand to gain
> a great deal from such an arrangement.

A long-term collaboration agreement with Siemens was signed in October 1974, under which TPI would manufacture precision press tools like stamping, forming, drawing and progressive dies for precision metal components, required in sophisticated telecommunications equipment. Siemens agreed to develop within TPI special carbide tooling, made of carbide steel that is denser and stronger than tool steel. This agreement was a significant advantage for TPI as Siemens deputed their Tool Room specialist, Reiner Fischer, to TPI to oversee operations in early 1975. He, too, played an important role in TPI's growth story. Siemens got an assured product at a pre-determined price, which they found favourable and the collaboration worked well. The arrangement proved to be a win-win for both the parties.

Expansion in Disk Drive Island

Change was happening at a scorching pace in the semi-conductor industry, and we had to devise strategies and methods to keep pace with these changes. TPI continued to upgrade itself to face global challenges.

With cost-cutting happening globally, companies like Texas Instruments and National Semiconductors decided 'to go East' to sub-contract their IC-manufacturing operations even though they had factories in Singapore, Malaysia and Indonesia. Though TPI did not possess IC transfer moulding technology, which was essentially an American proprietary knowledge, we pitched in to undertake spare parts building for these moulds, as maintenance support. The price was half of what US companies were offering, delivery was also faster as it was within Singapore. Soon, Texas Instruments and other semi-conductor companies like Smith Corona (for metal stamping dies) and Motorola started placing continuous orders with TPI. Gradually, our order book was looking more and more impressive. Our capacity was getting fully loaded, and we had to sub-contract some of our jobs for manufacturing mould bases to Larsen and Toubro in India.

I would send a monthly detailed report in a pre-fixed format to Moolgaokar. The report would carry details about technology, production, customers, quality control measures, costs and future business.

Moolgaokar replied meticulously to every letter which brought with it a new learning for all of us. When he wrote:

> I enjoy receiving your reports Syamal. Please also write to me about Singapore as a country, its economic policies, its people.

And when he also wrote: 'Pay major attention to minor details', it brought great lessons home. This was truly a golden period for me and TPI in Singapore.

While continuing with its focus on the semi-conductor industry, TPI was also getting into electro-mechanical jobs like computer peripherals, disc drives and printers. Ratan Tata, during one of his visits, also said that the time was right for TPI to get into electro-mechanical jobs.

The late 1970s and early 1980s saw the beginning of disk drive manufacturing in Singapore that was emerging as a major centre of disc drive industries of the world. This was an opportune moment for TPI to move into mass production of plastic parts for floppy drives. EDB introduced us to Seagate and Shugart of the US for supplying precision components for the manufacture of floppy disk drives (FDDs). For TPI, it was a smooth forward integration—from mould making to mass production of parts manufactured from these moulds. However, what was persistently challenging in the manufacture of precision parts for disk drives was to deliver to the customer, parts that were chemically clean. A greater challenge was to have minimal loose particles in these parts. The entire manufacturing line and handling of the parts at every stage of the process had to simulate a surgical lab. To facilitate this, TPI set up clean-room facilities for computer peripheral parts. Maintaining such high levels of hygiene was indeed unique to TPI.

Within a short period, Singapore's suppliers had increased mass production quantities from 5,000 per batch per month, to the level of a million drives per month. By the end of the 1980s, 80 per cent of the world's production of FDDs was in Singapore and the nation had gained fame as Disc Drive Island.

In the meantime, floppy disk drive makers in the US were soon moving up into the technology of hard disc drives (HDDs), with which data-storing capacity was increased multi-fold. FDDs were yielding to HDDs, which had more metal parts. This demanded mass production of metal parts rather than plastic ones. As precision machining was our forte, it was easy for us to take up mass production of metal machined parts. With our expertise in tool making, we built special purpose machines to mass-produce metal parts.

It was around this time that we happened to meet M.L. Tandon, chairman of Tandon Inc., for possible collaboration with TPI. The Tandons had decided to develop precision industry capability in Singapore and were willing to shift base and transfer its US operations to Singapore. They had realized that manufacturing parts in Singapore was far more competitive than importing them from the US.

One Sunday, the managing director of Tandon Inc., (which made floppy disk drives) requested Srinivasan, general manager, TPI, for some technical assistance. A team from Tandon Inc. met Srinivasan and others and requested them to build a tool suited for mass production on top priority. TPI rose to the occasion and was successful in making it. TPI became the second supplier of die-cast machined parts for Tandon.

From then on, TPI added precision metal machining as another division. It soon upgraded to building sub-assemblies of parts for Tandon. By 1990, TPI, which started as a tool-making company, transitioned into a precision mass production company serving Western Digital, Seagate and companies making similar products.

A Culture of Commitment and Challenging the Limits

The TPI team was known to never let down any customer who came seeking their assistance. Once, an Australian company approached us for building an injection-cum-blow mould. Though TPI did not have any special expertise beyond machining-to-drawing, we accepted the job and completed it successfully. The customer was ecstatic. Another client, Smith Corona, a typewriter manufacturer, was in urgent need of a metal stamping part, which was meant for 'fine-blanking', a process where components are finished while in the process of stamping. TPI accepted the order and supplied the parts with our own low-speed press. Smith Corona appreciated our efforts and transferred production of around 15 tools from another toolmaker to TPI.

Later, GE had a requirement for a metal stamping tool for a part made of beryllium copper. The specialty of the part was that it required a helix hole to be stamped. All along, GE had been trying to get a manufacturer in the US to make the tool. Many companies had already turned GE down; they did not want this job. When the purchasing engineer of GE, a British gentleman, approached TPI to take up the job, we accepted it as a challenge. GE was kind enough to give us a good price if the tool was successful. If, however, we did not succeed we would lose the cost of the tool. By now, TPI was used to taking on challenging tasks and, in fact, thrived on challenges. The job was done to the satisfaction of the GE engineer, who was so pleased with TPI's performance that he recommended TPI to be given first priority to participate in all GE's projects for tooling.

Another time, a large corporation from the US visited us. The company was looking for a big project and asked us for a quote for precision machining and moulding of some assemblies, electronics and connectors. Their financial controller was of Indian origin. We discussed the requirement and made a presentation to the company. They got back to us two days later saying that Hong Kong had agreed to do the job at half the price of what we had quoted. We explained the break-up of material and labour costs, trying hard to convince them that doing the job to the standards we delivered, half the price was simply impossible. They, however, did not accept our justification. Two years later, we received a frantic call from the same company asking us to make those parts. Apparently, the vendor to whom they had given the job was not able to deliver. We were only too happy to be of assistance!

Another occasion when we challenged the limits was in the latter half of 1974, when the electronic and semi-conductor industries faced a global recession and many large corporations in Singapore were forced to cut back production. A few electronic and semi-conductor companies had started laying off workers. This industry has always been very cyclical. The Singapore government was taking steps to keep the economy buoyant by way of reducing interest rates, lifting the credit squeeze, and by trying to hold the price line. Even so, many reputed local support manufacturers were facing serious difficulties.

Within two years of starting operations in Singapore, TPI had consolidated its position in the international market as a pioneering tool room of international standards. However, the tide changed for TPI too. Our customers requested us to cut down our open orders. They agreed to take in whatever we could deliver in six weeks' time, beyond which the orders would be cancelled automatically.

This is when the full impact of the global recession was felt. We were at a critical juncture. Just when we had commenced a two-shift operation and were required to run a third shift to optimize plant operations, bulk orders from the semi-conductor industry were in jeopardy.

On the records, TPI had orders for three months; but now we had to plan what the team could deliver within the next six weeks. Upon reviewing the order value, we felt that these were high-revenue orders and it was advisable to complete the full volume in six weeks' time. We took steps to plan and utilize all our resources to complete the jobs, and discussed the matter with all our technicians. We had their support, and all the jobs were completed within the pre-determined time limit. What a proud moment it was for every employee of TPI when one day prior to the deadline, all the open orders were completed, delivered and accepted by the customers.

The entire TPI team rose to the occasion and did us proud.

The worldwide recession would have impacted TPI severely, like all other tool rooms in Singapore, but for our heroic team which was dedicated and united in purpose. We realized that if we did not complete the jobs on time, there would be no money for our salaries. The recession put pressure on us to cut down costs and economize in all areas possible. The financial situation was getting tighter and uncertainties in the international market were showing no signs of clearing. A decision was made to relinquish the town office, and measures were taken to minimize consumption of utilities. A few expatriate staff was sent back to India, though with great reluctance, as they were doing extremely well, and we hoped to bring them back as and when necessary.

Through all this, the team's morale did not drop. Our executives and supervisors were fully aware of the difficult situation, and offered to take a 10 per cent cut in their salaries should it become necessary. Such was the sense of commitment in the team.

Funding from India

Topmost on my list of trials and travails would perhaps be arranging finance from India for all our activities and also for expansion. This was largely due to the exchange controls. Thus, during the initial days, we often faced problems in securing funds for suppliers' payments and even for payment of salaries. Farrokh Kavarana, managing director of Tata Zug, that held a stake in TPI, helped us out on many occasions following several telephonic arguments about funding. He showed good understanding of our plight and had a sharp mind to grasp the situation quickly. As our money problems became severe, I spoke to Dr Mehta. He suggested I get to Bombay House and then we could jointly call on JRD and Moolgaokar.

I soon arrived in Dr Mehta's corner room in Bombay House and noticed that for a major part of the time he was busy on the telephone, as he was receiving a lot of congratulatory calls. I did not understand why and interrupted him trying to bring into focus the issue of my funds, but he simply did not pay any attention. It was another hour-and-a-half, before he told me that he had been appointed as director on the board of Tata Sons Limited.

My mind however, refused to let go of my overburdening issues. He glanced at me and thought I looked too washed out. He pushed a tablet towards me saying, 'Take this Babu [that's how he referred to me at times with affection]. This is a vitamin pill. I must go for my first lunch as a director of Tata Sons. My secretary will organize a meal for you. I shall be back soon.' Anyway, I swallowed the tablet, and felt the stress ease away slowly.

Dr Mehta came back looking jubilant and happy. He asked me 'How do you feel Syamal? I told him I felt relaxed. 'You were very tired and agitated, so I gave you one to refresh you. You see, Bombay House is not an easy place to work. See the number of telephone calls and then there are stalwarts like J.R.D. Tata, Naval Tata, Sumant Moolgaokar, Adi Billimoria and Darbari Seth to deal with. It is very strenuous trying to juggle everyone. In Bombay House you may need to take three pills a day if you want to survive,' he said.

After a prolonged wait and a whole lot of anxiety for me, Dr Mehta said, 'Now Syamal, you come tomorrow with your problem and we shall see what we can do. I must leave now for my celebratory dinner.'

We had the meeting the next day. As I was convinced that TELCO, our parent company, would not be allowed to send funds to us in Singapore, I was armed with an alternative proposal. Moolgaokar, Dr Mehta, J.E. Talaulicar, managing director of TELCO, and Maira, all heard me patiently explain the Permanent

Resident Scheme as suggested by the EDB. They seemed to be aware of the scheme and advised me to try that route to raise the required funds.

Under this scheme, people who wished to stay permanently in Singapore had to deposit S$250,000 with the government or an approved industry for five years. Accordingly, Harmindar and Brothers, a Singapore company deposited its funds with the government for permanent residency and chose to invest in TPI. It brought me some relief on the funds front.

Catalyst for Joint Ventures and Diversification

From the very beginning it was felt that we should set up other joint ventures and operations with TPI, to generate higher revenues. This idea was driven by the fact that return on investment on a precision engineering tool room like TPI was low. However, using the tools manufactured by TPI for production of components and products for other industries could be much more profitable. Several proposals for joint ventures were thus explored.

Tata-Cope Allman: The first one to materialize was Tata-Cope Allman for marketing, and eventually manufacturing of Cope Allman aerosol valves in Singapore. Katkar was appointed CEO of the joint venture. He successfully implemented the project and started marketing the products in Singapore and other Association of Southeast Asian Nations (ASEAN) countries. The company, however, could not move ahead because aerosol valves were discontinued due to pollution issues.

TataB: Another venture was successfully initiated between TELCO and Tengku Ariff Bendahara, the prince of Pahang state, Malaysia, to set up a plant for the assembly of TELCO vehicles for the Malaysian market. Sometime in 1974, when we had moved to the new TPI building in Jurong Industrial Estate, I got a call from the office of Tengku Ariff Bendahara. I was informed that the Prince wanted to talk to me about a possible joint venture for an assembly of Tata vehicles for the Malaysian market.

However, when I sent a message to Moolgaokar that the Prince had approached us for a partnership, I was promptly advised not to proceed with the proposal, as Tata Motors had assured him that it was already negotiating a licence with another party in Malaysia that would come through soon. Two weeks later, I got a message from Moolgaokar asking me to go ahead with the discussion with Tengku Ariff Bendahara for a possible joint venture with Tata Motors. This joint venture would be the first assembly line outside the country if the Tatas got the go-ahead.

With Tengku's consent, I arranged for the team from Tata Motors to visit Pahang. Later, JRD, Nani Palkhivala and Moolgaokar too visited Pahang. I was present at the final meeting in Kuala Lumpur when the deal was finalized. On 21 November 1974, a joint venture was started between TELCO and Tengku Ariff Bendahara of Pahang. In 1977, Maira of TELCO Pune, was appointed as the managing director of TataB. It gives me great joy that the first assembly joint venture came up in Malaysia where TPI played a role, however small. Later, TPI also attempted to market Tata vehicles in Thailand and Indonesia.

As the Tatas' base in Singapore, TPI became the catalyst for joint ventures and for promotion of Tata companies in South-East Asia, such as the truck plant in Malaysia, Tata Consultancy Services (TCS) in Singapore, and for the several attempts Singapore Airlines made to set up a joint venture airline with the Tatas.

Stalwarts Lead by Example

Tata values are enduring. Every Tata stalwart lived his life guided by these values, be it JRD, Moolgaokar, Palkhivala, Naval or

Ratan Tata who are but a few of our role models of simplicity, integrity, accountability, diligence, perseverance and discipline—the foundation for success. They practised these values that not only led to success and helped build their clean reputation but also inspired others. JRD visited Singapore twice, once in 1974 and then again in 1982. Each visit filled us with tremendous passion to excel and at once we would feel as if all our problems were melting away in the light of his vision.

JRD was a thorough gentleman and simple in his ways. Everyone at the Shangri-La Hotel in Singapore would look up to him. He would never take a suite and would insist on paying for his room. He would even wash his own clothes. JRD had an inquisitive mind and would spend a lot of time with the workers at their machines and at the design boards. He would sit at the computer to understand the designs. He showed keen interest in the materials and in machine cutting techniques.

Every encounter with JRD and Dr Mehta had some learning for me, be it their interest in computerization in a time when India was still unexposed to automation or their values of compassion and consideration. There were some lighter moments too. For instance, in those days although it was difficult to get an appointment with Singapore's prime minister, LKY was always kind enough to meet with JRD. Once, JRD was visibly upset when we had taken an appointment for him to meet the Prime Minister. He felt that the Prime Minister was a busy person and we should respect the demands on his time. Dr Mehta, also present, immediately piped in that this was exactly what he had conveyed to me. Yet despite his instructions, I had gone ahead and taken the appointment. 'Shyamlal [JRD's endearing moniker for me], you must listen to Freddie,' JRD chided me gently. However, the meeting with the Prime Minister was fruitful and later, JRD said he had enjoyed it thoroughly. Instantly, Dr Mehta responded, 'It was I who told Syamal to take the appointment.' I was privy to such lighter moments between two great personalities.

Once, while crossing the street in Singapore, JRD asked Dr Mehta a few questions related to Indian statistics. He wanted to know the per capita power consumption and the number of villages in India. I was impressed with Dr Mehta's instant answers. The next day, JRD again enquired about the number of villages in India. I was surprised that Dr Mehta now gave out a different answer. I tried to draw his attention to the apparent error, but he abruptly gestured to me to remain quiet.

Later, in his own inimitable style, Dr Mehta put it across to me, 'Look Syamal, I am an economist not an engineer like you. Engineers see all measures in black and white. For engineers two plus two is always four. Economists may vary figures as per the circumstances. Definitions change, boundaries change, anything is possible. So, you see, whenever I talk to JRD, never interrupt.'

In addition to calling on the Prime Minister, JRD would also meet the chairman of EDB and Dhanabalan of DBS to discuss varied issues relating to EDB, globalization and upgradation of skills and technology. He also insisted on correct demeanour at all times. We once hosted a formal dinner in his honour in Singapore. When I went to pick him up, he indicated that as I was the host, I should be at the hotel. I responded that my wife and Dr Mehta were taking care of the guests, but he insisted that these were things I should learn. Such was his modesty and his insistence on appropriate demeanour and courtesy.

JRD inspired us a lot. Once, as he was getting off an Air India plane at Singapore, I saw him carrying his own bag. When I offered to carry it, JRD insisted on managing it himself. He displayed tremendous self-sufficiency, respect and regard for all those around him.

JRD's visit to TPI was an unforgettable day for the team. All employees were impressed with JRD's humility. When I offered him my chair in the office, he said with all humility, 'Shyamlal, you are the boss of this organization and this chair is yours. Only you should sit there.' He then sat in the visitor's chair across my table. Though his stay was only a few hours, he made it a point to meet all the employees.

JRD also visited the Technical Training Institute. Shaikh had contributed significantly in building it as one of the best technical training institutes in Singapore. JRD's visit to the Institute was a red-letter day in its history.

Another Tata stalwart, Moolgaokar was one of the greatest engineers India has produced—a man with far-sighted vision. An engineer with hands-on experience, he even had a workshop at his home. He was a man of few words and always wanted a quiet environment to work in. He paid great attention to detail and I have always tried to follow his advice to pay *major attention to minor details*. JRD and Moolgaokar had many traits in common; perhaps that is why they were great friends. We were lucky to get an opportunity to work with such great people.

I remember an interesting incident. Once we made a new progressive die, and sent pictures of it to Moolgaokar. We knew he would appreciate the intricacies of the job and the quality of the products we made. He wrote a letter congratulating me and my colleagues for doing such a great job, but in that picture there was one screw with its head a little blurred. He sent word through Qazi, 'Tell Syamal the job has been done very well, but I wish he would take care of that small detail.' That was some education and training we received in being meticulous and attentive to details.

While I was in Singapore, I thought Moolgaokar might be interested in meeting Prof. Hugh Ford, and introduced them. Like Moolgaokar, Prof. Ford too had a small workshop at his home where he had developed a full working model of a locomotive, which is today displayed in one of the railway museums in the UK. Prof. Ford started his career as an apprentice, and was a hard-core engineer. He worked in Great Western Railway in Britain and then studied further and went into research. Both Prof. Ford and Moolgaokar got along very well and became close friends. Moolgaokar later even visited Prof. Ford's cottage in the UK. Just like Moolgaokar, Prof. Ford too excelled in all that he took up.

Prof. Ford, who was younger than Moolgaokar, once told me, 'Syamal, if Sumant were in the US he would be the chairman of General Motors.' Coming from Prof. Ford, I realized this was no ordinary compliment. JRD picked up Moolgaokar when he was with ACC to TELCO, a company which he built from scratch to become the leading manufacturer of trucks in India.

During my trips to India, I would visit a number of Tata companies to understand their working and to see how we could create new business opportunities for them in Singapore. I was privileged to meet and interact with several senior directors of other Tata companies such as Palkhivala, Naval Tata, Adi Billimoria, Darbari Seth and Simone Tata.

Naval would often voice his desire for the relaxation of restrictions and barriers in Indian industry. He was a great admirer of Singapore, especially the manner in which Singapore had grown and prospered. He would reflect on how Singapore had transformed into a prominent player in the industrial world. He visited Singapore twice, and each time he was kind enough to visit TPI. Once we hosted a dinner in his honour. A number of top industrialists, businessmen and government officials who attended were deeply influenced by his charismatic personality.

Another unforgettable Tata leader I had the good fortune to interact with was Palkhivala. Let me recount here some of my meetings with him in Singapore, which have left an indelible mark on me. It was sometime in 1972, when I was just settling down in Singapore. I got a message from Dr Mehta informing me that Palkhivala would be arriving shortly in Singapore to discuss certain legal issues and business matters, possibly regarding land matters. There were certain intricate issues that needed to be resolved with our lawyers. On the appointed date, I received Palkhivala at Paya Lebar airport. He was dressed in casual attire, no suit or tie and with just one hand baggage.

This was the first time I was meeting Palkhivala. He enquired about Singapore, its possibilities, plans and vision. He obviously knew a great deal about Singapore. Palkhivala then asked me about the matter he had come to look into and I handed him a document—maybe around 150 pages. He appeared to be glancing through the document, and in 5 minutes handed the papers back to me. When I asked him, 'Sir, would you like to keep this document for your perusal?' he said, 'I have already gone through it.' I was shocked. I thought he had done a casual reading and would certainly need to go through it again. Next day, I found him waiting in the lobby and we went together for the meeting as planned with Shook Lin and Bok, a prominent legal firm in Singapore.

Palkhivala started out by enquiring about the problem areas, deep-diving and thoroughly discussing each point that was raised. I was amazed by how he could make meaningful sense and discuss 150 pages of documents with legal implications, after having leafed through them within such a short span of time. The meeting ended cordially with all the points resolved in a short period of time. He may have spent just a couple of hours on these issues, which had been going back and forth between the different parties in Singapore and Mumbai for quite some time. I had heard about Palkhivala's brilliance and his legal genius, but it was quite another experience altogether to see him in action.

I remember another such experience. TPI was a joint venture

with DBS and Sime Darby. At one point, Sime Darby wanted to pull out, as they felt that their other businesses were more profitable. The whole issue eventually went into litigation. As we could not come to a mutual understanding after several meetings, Dr Mehta, in consultation with JRD and Moolgaokar, requested Palkhivala to visit Singapore and help resolve the various outstanding issues.

Palkhivala flew in from Mumbai along with Dr Mehta. It was a long and tough meeting and the discussions centred on the implications and meanings of certain clauses and how to resolve them. Sime Darby wanted to exit amicably, but there were certain issues related to compliance. One of the most important points of this meeting was that Sime Darby was to arrive at a valuation at which they would exit. Palkhivala once again took charge of the situation. He chaired the meeting with great ease and displayed genuine interest to arrive at a solution. It was ultimately left to his brilliance to ensure that the matter was amicably resolved.

Indian VIPs Visit TPI

Besides Tata stalwarts, Indian dignitaries too visited Singapore and TPI during the mid-1970s. After all, TPI as the first Indian industry to be set up in Singapore, aroused some curiosity. Besides, these visits helped to create goodwill and attract other Indian businesses. Our visitors included the then commerce minister, Pranab Mukherjee and industry ministers, T.A. Pai and Nanaji Deshmukh. Deshmukh, in his immaculate dhoti and kurta and clean reputation, was one of the dignitaries everyone loved to meet.

Pai, accompanied by top officials from the ministries of Industry, Commerce and Finance, visited TPI and spent 45 minutes with us on 25 January 1977. The minister took a keen interest not only in the high-quality precision jobs we had undertaken, but also the marketing aspect of non-traditional products, which had so far not been done in India. He expressed great satisfaction at the high level of skill achieved by TPI and its success in penetrating sophisticated markets like the US, Switzerland and Germany.

Prior to his visit at TPI, Pai had met Singapore's Minister of Finance Hon Sui Sen, who complimented TPI's operations. In fact, he requested Pai, 'Give us a few more skill-intensive, capital industries like TPI.' Pai responded that he was proud of TPI.

The Indian High Commissioner had arranged Mukherjee's visit to our office and plant. He was accompanied by Piyush Mankad who later became the finance secretary. Mukherjee showed a lot of interest in the company and our products and services because it was 100 per cent export-oriented.

Once, I got an urgent message from the Indian High Commission and from Mumbai that a prominent dignitary from India, Murli Deora, was visiting Singapore. Deora was then the mayor of Mumbai; a promising young man with a great future in Indian politics. As the time at his disposal was short, I met him at the airport and as suggested by him, drove him straight to Jurong. He said he had heard a lot about Singapore's low-cost housing programme and mass construction projects and wanted to see them. He wanted to replicate that in Mumbai. I took him to Jurong Town Corporation, the Housing Development Board and other places too.

Faqir Chand Kohli and his wife Swarn Kohli visited Singapore in 1976 as part of the Institute of Electrical and Electronics Engineers (IEEE) delegation. Kohli is known as the founder of TCS; who built the company from scratch. He is a brilliant engineer from MIT, and has significantly contributed to Tata Power too. He is globally recognized in the computer industry and well known for his knowledge of science and technology. Above all, he is an outstanding technologist and a good human being who always helps others. I have personally benefitted greatly from his support and guidance. Kohli is also well connected with universities in India and abroad and has helped in upgrading many institutes in India. My wife and I first met Kohli in Singapore and we have been close ever since.

During our meeting, we discussed the possibility of TCS setting up base in Singapore. I introduced him to Chandra Das and Gopinath of Intraco Ltd., an international trading company owned by the Singapore government, and a joint venture was formed. Subsequently, Intraco entered into a 50:50 joint venture with TCS Mumbai. It was formed to provide computer systems consultancy and software services to a wide range of industries, including hotels and companies engaged in transport, shipping and public utilities. The newspaper also quoted Palkhivala, chairman, TCS, saying that the new venture would also train Singaporeans, thus helping alleviate the shortage of computer professionals. This software house became an important venture of the Tatas in Singapore.

The new venture got its first job worth US$1 million from a government department of Singapore. Much later, speaking at a meeting, Gopinath spoke about how TCS found it easy to get million-dollar contracts, but in the early days when he had got the first job for TCS, it was indeed tough. Since then, India's image has significantly enhanced.

Kohli played a big role in promoting computerization in Singapore. He was also made a Fellow of the Computer Society in Singapore. I worked closely with him when I was associated with TCS, Tata Infotech, Tata Elxsi and Tata Consulting Engineers (TCE) on returning to India in 1982 to take charge of TEL. Knowing my background in engineering, he would discuss with me the new areas into which industries were moving. Kohli wanted TCE to play a major role in power engineering, distribution and grid management where he would lend his support in moving ahead.

Being Tata Men in Singapore

I learnt more about the Tata Group while in Singapore than when I lived in India. In India, I knew only about TISCO and TELCO, but in Singapore, I was expected to know about all the Tata Group companies.

All Tata employees identify themselves closely with their companies and with the Group. It was not unusual for ordinary people to refer to us in Singapore as 'Tata men'. When I visited government offices and played host to many a visiting dignitary in Singapore, I was always recognized as the Tata Man.

One morning, Ratan and I were waiting in the lobby of the Imperial Hotel for our car to arrive. In a few moments, we heard an usher calling out, 'Tata your car has arrived.' Ratan approached the usher to ask if he was saying something to him. Pat came the reply, 'No Sir, I am calling out for Tata to tell him that his car has arrived,' all the time gesturing to me as if I was Tata. Ratan was amused and laughed.

As Tata men in Singapore, we subscribed to the Tata policy to participate wholeheartedly in the progress and development of the countries in which we operate. In 1975, Singapore had deputed a team of industrialists, at the invitation of US President Jimmy Carter, to visit Atlanta to strengthen trade and business between the two countries. I felt humbled to be included in this delegation. TPI was also a part of the 'toolmakers' delegation to Japan and Paris in the same year when Srinivasan represented us at both the conventions. The Japan trip was particularly an eye-opener for TPI, when we learnt of Japan's 'just-in-time' delivery methods.

Once TPI was planning to collaborate with a US party to enter the metal lead frames manufacturing business, a product required for the semi-conductor industry. While in the midst of discussions, I received a call from Moolgaokar informing me that Ratan had shared insights with him that this technology was changing fast and metal lead frames would soon be replaced by a new technology. He, therefore, advised that we should not enter this field.

Ratan often went to the US to look at emerging technologies. Once, in 1980, he called me up from San Francisco and said, 'Syamal I have got a very interesting project. It is the parallel processing of computers, developed by a group of engineering entrepreneurs, including Dr Thampi Thomas, Joe Rizi and others in San Francisco.' Ratan said that the PP machine was more efficient, faster and technologically superior as it worked by segmenting the computers CPU into receiving and processing that made it smaller in size and more powerful than a main frame computer of that day. 'This is a start-up project. Can we raise two million dollars for it?' Ratan asked. I contacted EDB and a few other banks. Eventually, one Singapore bank promised to help the Tatas.

Ratan flew from San Francisco to Singapore and explained to me what this new technology was about. He also shared it with the banks and with EDB. Moolgaokar and Kohli supported Ratan's efforts on this project even though a lot of people within and outside the Group tried to dissuade him, as the products were still under development. However, Ratan persisted and funding finally came from Tata Sons and Arthur Rock, followed by Hambrecht & Quist and Weiss Peck & Geer.

Ratan was considering using TPI as a base for assembling PP machines in Singapore. Certain operations were intended to be carried out in Singapore that marked the beginning of Tata Elxsi. My brother, Kajal, who worked with NASA, was passing through Singapore and I casually discussed the PP computers of Tata Elxsi with him. He studied this in-depth and found it interesting. On his return, he introduced Tata Elxsi to NASA. They were impressed and requested a presentation, as they neither knew about Tata

Syamal Gupta (seated second from left) as a student at Imperial College, London, 1963.

Syamal Gupta with J.R.D. Tata at the Ring Rolling Mill, Jamshedpur, 1971.

J.R.D. Tata planting a tree at Tata Precision Industries, Singapore (mid-1970).

Syamal Gupta with Professor Hugh Ford of Imperial College, London.

Syamal Gupta with N.A. Palkhivala and Farookh Kavarana at the Dewas leather plant in mid-1980s.

Sumant Moolgaokar (in grey suit) visits Tata Precision Industries, Singapore in the 1980s.

Syamal Gupta with Kenneth Kaunda, President of Zambia, at the Presidential Palace, 1984.

Ratan Tata with the then Deputy Prime Minister of Singapore, Lee Hsien Loong at the Tata Exports showroom, 1992.

Ratan Tata, group chairman, with Syamal Gupta and senior management team of McDonnell Douglas Helicopter at Arizona, USA, 1993.

Syamal Gupta (front row, seated second from right) at the Commemoration Day Function of Imperial College held at the Royal Albert Hall, London, 1993.

(L to R) AIG executives, Evan G. Greenberg, president and COO; Jon H. Chambreau, GM–Representative Office (India); and Maurice R. Greenberg, chairman and CEO, escorted around the Tata showroom by Syamal Gupta, 2 March 1997.

Syamal Gupta with Ratan Tata and Jamshed Irani at TISCO, Jamshedpur, August 1999.

Syamal Gupta with Dr Abdul P. J. Kalam, then President of India, at a CII function in Delhi, 2005.

Syamal Gupta with Ratan Tata and Thabo Mbeki, President of South Africa.

Syamal Gupta with the then British Prime Minister Gordon Brown at Tata BP Solar Plant.

Syamal Gupta, invited as guest of honour on Founder's Day, TISCO, Jamshedpur, 3 March 2009.

Elxsi nor about the availability of any such machine. Dr Thomas of Elxsi, one of the creators of PP machines, made a presentation to NASA. This was a success and later, NASA decided to purchase a machine. Elxsi sold a machine to NASA in 1984. This was also the year when Elxsi introduced the world's first symmetric multi-processor. The NASA order made everyone sit up and take notice of Elxsi for its powerful computers that could be used for advanced research or hi-tech computing. Soon, there was an order from Advanced Research Lab in Melbourne and Martin Marietta for the 'Star Wars' programme.

Lucky Country for Ratan: Following his frequent visits to Singapore, Ratan gradually realized the potential of the country. He also believed that Singapore was lucky for him. He would say, 'Syamal whenever I am in Singapore, I get some good news unexpectedly.' It was true. He received bigger responsibilities within the Tata Group, while passing through Singapore.

In August 1974, while visiting Singapore, Ratan, as director-in-charge of NELCO, was appointed director of Tata Sons; in August 1977, again while in Singapore, he was made director of TISCO; and in October 1991, he was appointed chairman of Tata Industries.

Thereafter, Ratan took up greater responsibilities. As chairman of Tata Sons and director of many companies, he became busy but he continued to make official visits to Singapore. Once in a while, he would joke, 'Syamal, let us go together to Singapore so that we can get some good news.'

Ratan is recognized as a successful industrialist globally. Singapore too recognized his contribution. He was appointed on the boards of EDB, Temasek, Singapore Airlines and many other organizations in Singapore. Many of his contacts from his earlier days in Singapore are still very strong.

On 29 August 2008, Tata Sons Directors, N.A. Soonawala and R.K. Krishna Kumar were in Singapore with Ratan when, in recognition of the contribution made by the Tata Group in building Singapore, the government conferred an extremely rare title of Honorary Citizenship on Ratan Tata, Chairman, Tata Sons Ltd. At the ceremony, Deputy Prime Minister Wong Kan Seng, described Ratan as being an exemplary business leader who had helped vitalize Singapore's economy. It was a great occasion at the State House and Ratan finally got a home in Singapore, which he so desired. Irrespective of the numerous distinguished honours conferred upon him worldwide, he continues to be his usual humble self.

At the same function, Nathan's ADC gave me a beautifully packed gift from the president. When I opened it, Krishna Kumar and Soonawala, who were also present at that moment, pointed out that the president had penned a message to me in his own hand. It read:

> With much appreciation for your abiding interest in Singapore
> and all that you have done over the years to promote Singapore
> as a place of business opportunity beyond the Tata family.

Strong Connections

My philosophy for management at TPI was simply based on the Tata principles. We were committed and kept our promises. I believed that all employees were equal irrespective of their varying levels of responsibility. I believed in an open-door policy. Everybody, be it a technician or a manager, had something worthwhile to contribute and it was my job to listen to them patiently and to mobilize everyone's involvement in the tasks at hand.

Empowerment comes with trust—trust in the individual's ability to deliver. I saw umpteen examples of my team living up to my confidence in them. Each time we had dignitaries visit TPI, be it JRD, Moolgaokar, Ratan or Kavarana, the concerned department head would present the daily running scenarios and I would stand behind him or her. Each time, the team made me proud.

I believe it was this trust that helped us to make constant improvements in productivity and it was this culture of continuous productivity improvement that was the primary driver for expanding our business. I was happy to be able to make my contribution in building TPI.

I met S.R. Nathan, who held senior positions in various ministries in the government of Singapore and later became the chairman of The Strait Times in 1982. He was a magnetic personality and his admirable qualities saw him rise to become Singapore's ambassador to the US. On his return, he was appointed Ambassador-at-Large and concurrently director of the Institute of Defence and Strategic Studies at the Nanyang Technological University. He often mentioned TPI to foreign visitors as a Singapore company that was doing well.

I was delighted when Nathan became the president of Singapore. I met him at Istana—his official residence in Singapore—as a core group member of the Confederation of Indian Industry (CII) delegation. Once when I called on him with Ratan and Muthuraman, managing director, Tata Steel, he expressed his joy at seeing us and recalled the Tatas' contribution in Singapore. He recounted how all official overseas visitors to Singapore would be directed to TPI with the express purpose of showing them the technology that resided in the country.

As I recount all those people who helped us, the name of Ng Pock Too, the young desk officer at EDB stands out prominently. His perseverance and determination to see the Tatas come into Singapore and the efforts that he put in to back it all up, are most commendable. His work was also much appreciated by his seniors in Singapore.

Another person who supported us in Singapore was Thomas Abraham, a young Indian Foreign Service (IFS) officer, who was the Indian High Commissioner to Singapore. He was known for his honesty, integrity and commitment to build the India–Singapore relationship. Though his role demanded more of a diplomatic focus, he went out of his way to support trade and industry. Abraham would enlighten us on how important Singapore was for India and South-East Asia. The need to protect the Andaman Islands, which are just 80 km away from Indonesia, often featured in his exchange. Others who supported and participated in my Singapore journey were Siddharth Acharya and Das Gupta, High Commissioners to Singapore, who were always co-operative as were Ratnakar Rao and B.M.C. Nair from the Indian Embassy.

Till today, Nathan, Chan Sek Keong, the former chief justice of Singapore, Pock Too and many others from Singapore are still in touch with me after all these years. Chan Ching Bok of EDB; Gopi Pillai, general manager, Intraco; and Chandra Das, managing director, Intraco—all continue to remain friends.

A Trail-Blazing Transformation

Looking back, the Singapore of the 1970s when I first landed and the Singapore of today have many a story to tell. Singapore transformed rapidly before my eyes from a third-world nation to a first-world nation within a definite span of time. It has grown over the years in terms of trade, industry, business, as also in terms of human development and entrepreneurship. Free and fair trade practices and the free market economy helped the country as did the thought process of the Singapore government that if the country had educated and skilled people, they would be employable and would contribute to society. Thus, housing, education and medical services are the backbone of social life and the government took it upon itself to provide the best-in-class services in all these three areas to its citizens.

Education was a priority and Singapore spent a lot of money on it. New schools were set up and existing ones were upgraded. There was a lot of emphasis on higher education and training. Efforts were made to upgrade the Nanyang Technological University, which went on to count as one of the top 100 universities in the world. Top students were given an opportunity to study at the National University of Singapore or sent abroad. Hundreds of students went to the UK, the US, Canada and Australia to get the best education possible. The government also did not give up on the school drop-outs. They were trained to be productive and capably participate and effectively contribute to the Singaporean society. Able-bodied people who did not get a chance to go to university could go to polytechnics where they were offered diploma courses. Today, Singapore boasts of 100 per cent literacy. The government promoted meritocracy in a big way and that contributed significantly to the Singaporean society.

Singapore always strived to create a better tomorrow for its citizens. Locals said Singaporean society was based on '1, 2, 3, 4'. It meant 1 wife, 2 children, a 3-bedroom house and a 4-wheeler. That was the way the nation wanted its citizens to move forward. This was no government dictum, but the campaign caught the imagination of its citizens and that is the profile of a Singaporean you see today—a healthy family composition. This is what the government promoted in a subtle way that worked wonders.

Ecology was another prime concern. Greenery was preserved and even enhanced and pollution control was managed wonderfully and sustained till date. Even as Singapore changed, it took great care and cautions to maintain its heritage. Old buildings from the time of Japanese occupation were restored. The real work was done by LKY and his highly capable and star-studded team. The LKY government realized that the country could make good progress if professionals joined politics. Their knowledge and competence would be made available to the government and their time devoted aptly to the people of their constituency. Proven people were inducted into government posts. Gautam Banerjee, chairman of Price Waterhouse Corporation, was an Indian origin Singaporean who was nominated to be a Member of Parliament (MP). Pock Too, who was with the EDB, was recognized as a successful individual and rose to become an MP to serve the Singapore government. Yow Chow Tong, also from EDB, was a successful professional engineer who joined politics and became a minister. A few people came from the grassroots to support the party. This was the biggest HR exercise that the government successfully implemented under LKY's leadership.

Some years ago, when LKY visited India, he addressed a select gathering of people, and mentioned how even at the retirement age, he was continuing to contribute. 'It is not a question of working or retirement,' he remarked. 'What matters is that one should be relevant to society. One must try to be relevant. If you are not, train yourself and develop yourself.'

Today, Singapore is a launch pad into South-East Asia for Indian businesses and an integral market and hub for the Tata Group of companies. The Asia-Pacific headquarters of TCS and offices of Tata Communications, NatSteel Holdings, Tata Technologies, Voltas, Tata Chemicals, Tata Power, Tata NYK Shipping, Kalzip Asia (a division of Tata Steel Europe), Tata Capital and York Transport Equipment (Asia), among others, are located in the island state. With all of these subsidiaries here, the Tata Group is a considerable creator of jobs with an employee base of over 2,000 people in Singapore.

While Singapore occupies a very special place in my heart, as Singapore was being rebuilt, my thoughts often flew to Jamshedpur city, which was also developed on similar lines. With its wide roads, good electricity, airport, hospitals, schools and disciplined labour force, Jamshedpur is a great place. It was built over 100 years ago and while there has been a lot of encroachment by private parties, yet Tata Steel city has remained a beautiful place.

Time to Move On

TPI as a start-up green-field project proved to be a great success. In a short space of time, TPI earned global recognition and was able to work with global leaders in high-tech industries. The pioneering spirit of the Tatas beckoned them to look beyond national boundaries to go global much before the world started taking globalization seriously. They were the pathfinders for Indian industry. Thence, TPI was conceptualized. TPI went on to prove that when decisions are born out of national good and backed up by untiring and ground-breaking actions, success is simply a foregone conclusion.

TPI is the handiwork of one of India's most worthy sons, Moolgaokar, whose demonstrated engineering brilliance was beyond compare. What drove TPI was the penchant and the dedication of its 150 engineers, technicians and business professionals who chose to tread the path less trodden, and they left behind them a trail for many others to follow—in Singapore and in India.

Mild India Fever

P.V. Narasimha Rao, former prime minister of India, during his visit to Jakarta, Indonesia, in September 1992, to attend the Non-Aligned Movement (NAM) Summit, met Prime Minister Goh Chok Tong of Singapore. They discussed cooperation between Singapore and India and mutually decided that they will promote the India-Singapore business partnership on a bigger scale. Subsequently, there were discussions between Singapore and India, followed by visit of trade missions of both countries to explore possibilities for bilateral cooperation and joint ventures in a number of businesses.

Goh Chok Tong was very committed to this bilateral business relationship and announced at his National Day Rally speech in August 1993 that he will visit India shortly where he wants to start a 'mild India fever', signalling a strong relationship between the two countries. He took great interest to increase significantly bilateral trade. Singapore-India bilateral relationship has grown stronger by the year on the signing of the Free Trade Agreement.

Later, Goh Chok Tong visited India as prime minister of Singapore. I was part of the CII core group of South-East Asia and Singapore and was part of the delegation that met him at the Taj Mansingh Hotel, New Delhi. The meeting hall was fully packed.

Prime Minister Goh gave a very passionate speech about how Singapore has grown in terms of trade, industry and business, as also in terms of human development and entrepreneurship. He said it had been possible because of free and fair trade practices and the free market economy. He further urged India to open up its economy and made a tremendous pitch towards this possibility.

In that meeting, it became clear that many Indians held senior positions in Singapore. This was possible because of the open policy of the government. Goh said that there was no underemployment but in fact there was over-employment. The GDP too had grown significantly.

I was greatly impressed with Goh's speech and to know that he played a significant role in bringing Singapore and India together. He promoted India a lot in Singapore and started the 'mild India fever' campaign.

Prime Minister Goh was a soft-spoken, reserved, decent and humble person. There is a saying in Singapore that while Prime Minister Lee Kuan Yew had a balanced head, Prime Minister Goh Chok Tong had a good heart.

Call of a Fresh Responsibility

With TPI successfully operating out of Singapore and with many lessons learnt over 10 years, the Tatas felt it was time for me to venture into uncharted waters once again. One morning, sometime in mid-1981, I received a telephone call from B.K. Bose, public relations officer of TELCO, Mumbai, requesting me to meet Moolgaokar, their chairman.

Assuming that it was a matter pertaining to TPI, I took a flight to Mumbai and arrived straight at the head office where I met Talaulicar. He had always been good to me, right from my days at TISCO, in the Ring Rolling Mills. He said Moolgaokar was waiting for me in his office and had some important matters to discuss.

I met Moolgaokar who was ensconced in his well-appointed chair and was calm and quiet as always. He looked like an erudite professor and welcomed me warmly. He told me that I had done a good job with TPI during the 10 years I had been in Singapore. He mentioned that the managing director of Tata Exports Limited (TEL) was taking up another assignment and the post was now vacant. He further asserted that India needed to globalize and promote export, due to its difficult foreign exchange situation.

Though TEL was doing well, it needed to do much more towards achieving greater profit margins and higher turnover. He emphasized that I had gained good experience with companies in the US, the UK and other countries during my stint in Singapore. This had led the Group to decide I would be the ideal person to return to India and take charge at the helm of Tata Exports. Moolgaokar told me that I was shortlisted to lead the Group's businesses in view of my varied international exposure and experience.

Moolgaokar also pointed out to me that after living and working in Singapore for 10 years, it would be challenging to relocate to

India, particularly in terms of accommodation and schooling for my children. To that end, he assured me the company would help me so that the transition would be smooth. I could tell that he really wanted me to come back and take over TEL. He said he was confident that I would be able to transform the company into a leading international business house.

Later, I met Palkhivala, then chairman of Tata Exports, who briefed me on the company. Leather was being manufactured from a new plant, along with transmission line towers and other businesses. On Palkhivala's advice, I met JRD who said he had discussed my appointment to this challenging job with his colleagues. He felt that dealing with government departments and controls could be difficult but I would be able to handle the task. He advised me to try manufacturing high-value products for exports to international markets.

I had barely stepped out of JRD's office when I bumped into my colleagues from Tata Motors, Guru Bhat and Balagopal. I had worked with Balagopal on an Indonesian project for Tata Motors Export division and with Bhat for development of a Malaysian project. They too had heard about my new appointment and agreed that it would be good for me to return to India at this stage. I also had a chat with Maira, my old friend from TISCO. He too was aware of my shifting base and shared with me the challenges in Tata Exports and the need for promoting exports in a big way. I also spent a couple of evenings discussing the offer with Ratan. He too was aware of my probable return to India on this new assignment. We discussed the pros and cons of this crucial move.

TEL was a prestigious company in the early 1980s, as it was into exports—an area that the government was vigorously promoting. But many of my friends and business associates from Singapore told me that since I had spent 10 critical years in Singapore's development, I should stay back and carry on with the work we had begun at TPI. They insisted that I could achieve a whole lot more personally and professionally for the Tatas by operating from Singapore. This advice did influence me. However, I always knew that the Tatas had deputed me to Singapore to do a job, which I believe I had done to the best of my ability, and it was not my prerogative to stay back. Rather, it was imperative that I return to India when the Tatas wanted me.

I returned to Singapore and discussed the matter with my wife and family members and they were happy with the news. After a fortnight of meetings with seniors at the Head Office, I informed Moolgaokar that I had decided to return and take over the assignment at TEL (now Tata International Ltd).

It was time to say au revoir to beautiful Singapore and to my 150-strong team who were family first, and then colleagues. It was also time to bid adieu to friends and supporters in the government, in industry and in every sector of Singapore who gave me wonderful memories to take home. It was time to say 'thank you' once again to the Tatas for the opportunity, trust, confidence and the support to bring ideas to reality, and it was now time to consider new opportunities, new challenges, new pathways and new vistas. It was time to move on.

I left Singapore with a feeling of contentment that the entry of TPI 10 years ago was followed by many other Tata businesses and several other Indian businesses which had successfully established themselves and worked alongside the Singapore government. I took on my next assignment with the Tatas back in Mumbai.

Chapter 5

GOING INTERNATIONAL

I returned to Mumbai and visited TEL's Head Office at Shivsagar Estate at Worli, Mumbai. TEL was an entity created by TELCO under Moolgaokar's direction. Several TELCO engineers and managers had then moved to TEL and one of their major export businesses was Tata vehicles. I was introduced to all the department heads in the TEL office. I knew some of the gentlemen, particularly those who had previously worked for TELCO. The others were, of course, new to me. I also met Hoshie Malgham, the chief financial officer, with whom I had an encounter once, while I was with Tata Steel. We did not start off on the right foot and the story of that meeting with Malgham makes for interesting reading.

It was in June 1970, when Moolgaokar had arranged to send me and some other executives to South-East Asia to explore business and investment opportunities. I went under the blanket foreign exchange permit granted to Tata Exports in those days by the government of India and I was not aware about the requisite rules and regulations. I took foreign exchange from TEL because the visit was for export promotion.

On my return from the trip, even as I was busy preparing my visit report, I got a message from TEL to immediately submit my travel expense statement. I took this communication a bit lightly and replied that I will do the needful in a few days' time.

Another reminder followed shortly until finally I received an ultimatum from Moolgaokar's office saying, 'Syamal, please submit your foreign travel expense report, which is necessary under the government's foreign exchange rules and regulations. Visit Mumbai and sort it out immediately.'

I went to Mumbai and was sent to meet Malgham, then the chief accountant of TEL, who also looked after Legal and Secretarial. He was with TEL since its inception and played a key role in opening offices in Hong Kong and Africa. I could see his visible annoyance at my not submitting the foreign travel bill. He told me, 'Do you realize the responsibility of Tata Exports in giving you foreign exchange and the implications of you not submitting the expense report? Only a few companies have got this blanket permit under which they can send their executives abroad so long as it is in the interest of the company and has long-term export potential.' He told me to submit the travel expense report immediately, which I did. I had not met him since that day, more than 12 years had passed. We started on a fresh slate. After a few more back and forth visits to settle everything, I finally returned from Singapore to Mumbai in January 1982 and took charge of TEL as its managing director.

A Trading House under Pressure

I found that unlike other export houses, TEL was well-managed and striving to become a superstar trading house in response to the government of India's keenness to promote exports. India's external trade at that time was US$8 billion and the government was encouraging exports to offset India's precarious balance of payments position. To make international trade and business self-sustaining, the need for setting up export houses was felt in a big way. However, companies just did not have the scale, connections or the resources to promote international business.

The rupee-dollar exchange rate was around 6 to 8 rupees to the dollar and travelling abroad, even for business promotions, was difficult. Without a dedicated marketing organization, the cost of exports of individual Indian companies was disproportionately high as compared to their export turnover. The government understood the need for removal of trade restrictions, but was trapped with its conflicting sets of priorities because of historical reasons. It therefore supported the trading house concept, where one company could represent a number of medium- and small-scale firms in international markets.

Tata Exports was thus incorporated in 1962 as a general trading division by the legendary expert in international trade and export-import, B.S. Bhatnagar along with P.A. Narielwala under the overall guidance of Moolgaokar. Bhatnagar as the general manager of TEL, had a good working relationship with the government and could approach any department for clarifications. He was of valuable support to the Tatas and always worked to promote industry.

Even as trade bodies and export organizations were preparing long-term plans for the growth of international business, the government began to offer sops like tax subsidies, for those who want to travel for export promotion. However, the hard facts remained— there were barely any Indian products and services available for exports. As there was little globalization, Indian manufacturers produced mainly for local consumption and these products were hard to market internationally.

TEL however, had a wide range of products, services and a number of representative offices abroad, entrusted with a huge responsibility for exports. It had a list of approved vendors for different products and quality control was monitored by its own staff. Today, while most major Tata companies manage their own exports, trading houses can still play a better role in countries to which exports are lower. TEL's major businesses were trading, transmission line towers, leather and leather products, chemicals and fertilizers, steel, auto, marine products, pumps and agricultural machinery. It was usual then for a trading house to operate with a wide range of products as customers preferred to buy varied products from a single source. Also, not many foreign businesses would come to India in those days due to its restrictive trade practices and investment climate.

On taking charge, I studied the organizational structure of Tata Exports and its various businesses. I evaluated the existing set-up of the company which was backed by strong services such as product marketing; identifying customers, besides arranging and utilizing the line of credit, handled by a special cell that also provided legal and secretarial services. The company also provided exchange advisory services to guide operating departments on country risks. I, however, noticed that the import-export business was a different ball game altogether from other conventional businesses, and needed extra attention bearing in mind the Foreign Exchange Regulation Act (FERA) later replaced by FEMA regulations of the government, which had to be followed as per their set guidelines.

For instance, when I delved deeply into the regulations of trading as laid out by the government, I learned that 10 per cent of the products for export needed to be sourced from the small- and medium-scale industries, which led us to the business of carpets, considered as a cottage industry. In addition, to keep our trading house licence active, we had to grow at the rate of 10–15 per cent every year.

We had to make the best of what we had and learn to navigate as best as possible the labyrinth of export rules and regulations that controlled Indian businesses. In this scenario, there emerged a lot of pressure from the government to reach out to the outside world. Due to our long-standing cordial cultural ties with Africa, the Indian government was trying to promote Indian business to these countries. The government also invited several African delegations to visit India to promote diplomatic relations and explore business opportunities.

Global business, however, meant international quality of products and handling the job effectively in terms of quality, productivity, delivery, pricing and after-sales service. These were factors with which India was still grappling. TEL was learning to match these criteria and to become a leading player in the international market.

Drafting an Export Strategy

The rationale in India those days were, 'we export because we have something in surplus,' but we at TEL tried a different approach. We felt we had to have the right products and services that we could offer to other countries and only then exports would work. I would thus often reach out to Ratan, whose contacts around the world were growing. We often discussed the performance of big companies in the US and in other parts of the world and about advancing technologies. He also supported my efforts to get into high-tech areas.

I also attended the first board meeting at TEL and was quite overwhelmed to meet the members. Palkhivala was the chairman and the others included Moolgaokar, Naval Tata, Pallonji Mistry, director of TEL and Tata Sons and D.R. Pendse, chief economist of the Tatas. I was happy to be associated with a company that was managed by eminent group members who were all legends in their fields.

Palkhivala's broad vision for the company was to be a major player in the international market. Moolgaokar spent a lot of time explaining his views about trading houses and expected TEL to follow the practice of Japanese trading houses while operating within our local limits. He was familiar with Japanese industrial practices and felt that Tata Exports, which was already following a similar model, would grow into a major player internationally. I found that one of the strengths of Japanese trading houses was a wide network of offices across the globe. Mitsubishi had 200 offices worldwide while we had only a couple of them. I needed to change this. We started representative offices and companies overseas to promote our international businesses.

Palkhivala's view on exports was that it was not only a foreign exchange earner for the country, but provided us an opportunity to learn about competitors—their pricing strategy, management skills and strengths. Ultimately, this knowledge would enrich our organization. It would be helpful in training our own people in gradually becoming important players in the global market.

As planned, I would meet Palkhivala every month to review the progress of the company and to discuss other matters of importance such as government policies, rules and regulations. It was also important to keep the chairman informed about our entry into new markets and countries, more so in Africa. Palkhivala always came to our Worli showroom when foreign dignitaries visited us. I also kept him informed about the company's operations and regularly sought his guidance.

Similarly, I also regularly updated Moolgaokar about the highlights of TEL's operations and on our move to bring in new technology and new locations. Moolgaokar was happy to receive first-hand knowledge about all international operations, the ensuing issues and new learnings from each country. He was always keen to discuss emerging technology and our entry into new businesses like solar, float glass, insurance, aviation and other fields which we were evaluating.

Organizations are always as effective or as good as the people they have and my first job at TEL was to understand the team. I would regularly meet the staff members, first in groups and then individually, trying to understand their task and the role they were playing, how they were performing and where I could be of assistance and guidance. This was a new task for me and opened up opportunities for new ideas.

I also shared my experiences in international business and discussed new ideas with my colleagues. We felt there was a need to send staff members to international business meets and soon started sending senior executives to universities and business schools abroad for specific programmes. We encouraged colleagues to apply for competitive scholarships. We started interacting closely with Mitsubishi, introduced Japanese language courses, encouraging employees to learn to speak, read and write the language.

I also believed in the all-round well-being of employees. It was important that every employee was engaged in indoor or outdoor sports activities. So we set up badminton facilities at a local gymkhana, encouraged swimming, and classes for martial arts and yoga.

Development of Divisions

In India, our methods, business environment and ideologies were different from other developed countries. In an open economy, consumers have a choice to buy as per their exact needs. So, in order to be a global player and to remain competitive, I figured one had to put more resources into product development and R&D. I decided to expand our presence in target countries. TEL those days had two manufacturing units and one contracting set-up.

The leather finishing unit and the footwear and garments division were on the manufacturing side, and the Transmission Line Towers (TLT) was on the contracting side. I was in touch with each and every division, including TELCO, and promised our full support in all activities. We functioned as the TELCO division of TEL in all our overseas transactions.

Speeding Up Vehicle Sales Overseas: One of TEL's major lines of business was Tata vehicles. TELCO realized that exports needed to be promoted in order to get products and services up to international standards. We were exporting Tata vehicles to the Middle East and South-East Asia and to one entry point in Africa, in addition to Nepal, Bangladesh and Sri Lanka. I felt my first job was to try and encourage our vehicle sales in other countries. After all, these vehicles were symbolically our flag bearers and significantly increased visibility for our business. This required understanding the competition abroad and upgrading our vehicles to be competitive, wherever necessary. I was well-acquainted with people from TELCO, now Tata Motors, who supported me when I joined as managing director.

We figured that while our markets were limited in South-East Asia, Tata Motors continued to have greater presence in the Middle East and Africa. Eventually, it was felt that in order to achieve customer proximity and to take advantage of better conditions, such as an enabling political environment, the Tatas had to start manufacturing units closer to the markets. The assembly plant for Tata Motors in South Africa was an example.

Moolgaokar called me once in a while to enquire about international trade and business, how we were doing and how TEL fared internationally. He was keen to know about the performance of Indian products in international markets, especially Tata trucks, and how our trucks were performing in various countries in Africa. He would enquire in terms of price, after-sales service and perception in overseas markets compared with other major branded products. He would tell me to meet Tata Motors executives in Pune. He regularly visited Pune during weekends to get first-hand knowledge about the operations and often discussed the future plans of the company. He would sometimes invite me to accompany him to the Pune Plant.

This was how I learnt more about Tata Motors' operations and the people associated with the company. This was very useful for me in promoting Tata Motors abroad. Although I did not have the opportunity to work with Moolgaokar earlier, as I was away in Singapore, I worked closely with him after returning to Mumbai when he shared his views on projects, technology and people.

Powering Up TLT Exports: The TLT division exported transmission line towers, used to support overhead power lines. As TLT fabrication work was reserved for the small-scale sector, TEL promoted Jyoti Structures, as a small-scale industry in which it held a minority shareholding, to complete the fabrication jobs. Operations were overseen by the TEL team. This division was well organized with its own design and marketing capabilities and promised some big opportunities. The TLTs were exported to Sri Lanka, Thailand, the Philippines, Egypt, Iran and Indonesia, while sub-station equipment and works were executed in Sudan, Iraq, Mauritius, Algeria, Dubai and Sri Lanka.

Mr Maneck Hiranandani was the director-in-charge of this division and he did a splendid job to build this business and he was ably assisted by P.N. Dhar.

Moolgaokar had helped in setting up the TLT division. He realized that the pricing of steel angles and channels was controlled by the JPC. However, if this export item was used as a manufactured product, one could charge market prices, that were inflated and higher than the controlled prices. It was the typical Japanese model—export products and services where you have some in-depth knowledge so you can service customers well and get better returns.

In the Indian market, the main purchasers of TLTs were public sector enterprises such as National Thermal Power Corporation, Power Grid Corporation of India and numerous state electricity boards. In 1998, the division found a good alliance partners in Loxley Inc. and TEDA in Thailand, promoting the business locally. We were in a unique position as far as the TLT business was concerned because we had our own design and fabrication facility.

The TLT business had consistently done well and was ranked among the top three in India in the 1980s. With jobs in India and abroad executed successfully, it was subsequently handed over to Tata Power and then to Tata Projects as per the restructuring recommendation of the internal consultants as approved by the Group's top management. We added another business unit as part of TLT—railway electrification, which was big in those days and perhaps even today.

Growing Farm Machinery Sales: We exported agricultural machinery such as pumps, tractors, power tillers, sprinklers and also steel under TEL's Agricultural and Construction Machinery division. The idea was that when you go to a country to sell pumps, they may ask for something else along with it—like the base of the pumps or some steel parts. In this way, you could package products for export. R.L. Das was responsible for this division and he did a good job!

There is a big demand for these products in Zambia even today, where we have a company dedicated to sale of agricultural equipment. Several years ago, when I was in Addis Ababa, Ethiopia, along with the Prime Minister's delegation for the Africa Mission conference, I heard Sanjay Kirloskar, the prominent Indian industrialist, telling a small gathering that 25 years earlier, it was the Tatas that promoted Kirloskar pumps in Ethiopia and they are still doing good business in the country.

However, my main objective was to steer the company's growth into more sophisticated manufacturing and engineering sectors, to broaden its technological base and increase the share of its own manufactured products. Efforts were made for modernization, expansion and diversification of existing industries to enter high-technology sectors like computer peripherals, solar energy systems and automotive ancillary industries.

I endeavoured to keep myself abreast of technological developments through visits to various industries and also by maintaining contacts with experts in their respective fields.

Deepening the Marine Segment: We were also into marine products which went on to become a lucrative business as there was substantial demand for seafood like prawns, pomfret and frog legs. We were led by the view that there would always be a demand for traditional products like rice and pulses, but we needed to move into the higher value-added products category for which we would need trained personnel. We therefore inducted graduate engineers and trained them in marine and sea product categories at TEL. The Fishery division was managed by Amar Sridharani. He would buy from the local markets and process the fish for exports. In order to expand our reach, Amar was posted in New York where he promoted seafood products. He continued to be involved with export promotion of marine products even after he returned to India. In fact, we were also involved with shrimp cultivation in some parts of India and started to use our own brand, Jaltara, for high quality rice and pulses as we slowly gained experience in this business.

Infrastructure Services: For our Project Equipment & Service division, I took a keen interest in guiding the teams in projects relating to the steel and engineering industries. This division that exported cement plant equipment sourced from India, was headed by Naresh Chhabra, an ex-ACC man and an expert in the cement industry. There was a big requirement for cement plants in India and abroad. Chhabra had obtained a contract from Iraq for managing two cement factories by providing the technicians and required staff. He also promoted similar projects in Nigeria and other African countries. He infused a lot of enthusiasm in the staff. This division did well under his leadership.

Textile Trade: From its early days, textiles were an important area of exports. TEL sourced good-quality fabrics in-house from Tata Textiles. However, when I visited some of the leather and textile plants in Europe, I soon realized that there were deeper opportunities for us in the Indian sub-continent. Although Europe manufactured top-class products, mass production in textiles, garments and leather had to move to China, India and other Asian countries, where costs and labour were cheaper. Eventually, we felt it was too restrictive to only export Tata Textile products and started a parallel textile division to export textiles manufactured by other Indian companies.

During my tenure, Noel Tata joined TEL as an executive and restarted the textile and garment departments that were closed down earlier due to competition. He developed that business progressively.

Basket of Imports: TEL as a trading house was also involved in import of raw materials to fulfil the needs of the Tatas and other Indian companies for export production. Malgham headed this Imports division. We were allowed to import all the raw materials necessary for export production and also certain restricted items, against exports. Additionally, as an incentive, trading houses were given licences to import some products and to market them in India to generate revenue. With the passage of time, Malgham played a key role in developing businesses overseas and building relationship with other Group companies.

The Import division was an important part for TEL. For the import of restricted items, TEL sold import licences to actual users.

These parties imported items on our behalf and marketed them to book profits. There were premiums on the licences also, but more often, we imported special steels, ball bearings and other products for Tata Motors. Since we had dutyfree import licences, the company would ask us to get some products from China like steel, wheel rims, batteries and air conditioners. That was a good business which was eventually taken over by Tata Motors.

Our imports were worth crores of rupees so we had to be careful to cover exchange loss and provide for shipping and freight forwarding. We imported pulses, steel bearings and a variety of other items besides coal and oil that came into our trade basket by coincidence.

One day, I received a call from my contacts at British Petroleum (BP), London, saying that a Tata company was involved in a court case and arbitration in the UK. To them, all Tata companies were the same. When I enquired internally, I was informed that there was a dispute between BP and Tata Power and the former was going to sue the Tata company for not lifting the coal and paying demurrage.

BP had engaged two well-known barristers. I spoke to Dr Homi Sethna, chairman of Tata Electric Companies and to his executive assistant, K. Rajan, and convinced them and BP to arrive at a mutual arrangement rather than allow ego and personal issues to come in the way. A mutual agreement on compensation was reached and the matter was settled amicably.

Another interesting story revolves around how we procured import of coal and oil for Tata Power. Dr Sethna suggested that we should engage a third party to manage the imports which was a better practice, because a trader who does the import can offer a better price and add in shipping services too. This was how we were asked to handle their import as a trading house.

J.K. Niyogi and Noel Tata handled this job well and ensured

reasonable cost savings. There were no complaints about quality, source or price of coal. We invited open tenders with our recommendation of the price and shipping. All this expertise was developed in TEL and finally, the decision was with Tata Power to choose the party for import.

It is on record that Tata Power was happy with the services offered by TEL and they suggested that the facilitation fee of 1 per cent be increased to 2 per cent. Later, following a change in management in Tata Power, they decided to import the coal directly and became a trader of the commodity.

My belief was that the future would be in energy and we should tap into it. I consulted British Petroleum and Mitsubishi, and started a division for coal energy.

Leather Plant: On taking charge at TEL, one of my first priorities was to visit the Leather Finishing Plant at Dewas, Madhya Pradesh, which was not doing too well. It was a new business and had still not picked up pace. I had visited the Plant earlier when it was inaugurated. At the time, it was Moolgaokar's vision to make leather business an organized sector in India as against being run as a small-scale industry replete with erratic standards and practices. There was big potential in the leather industry.

Around that time, the Madhya Pradesh government was looking into ways to improve the lives of the people in their less-developed districts like Dewas, 40 km from the old historical city of Indore, which was an ill-maintained rural outpost with no approach roads or industries.

TEL leased from the state government 100 acres of land on one side of the road and 80 acres on the other side and the leather plant was developed in the same way as TELCO would put up a factory. With technical assistance from the Italians, TEL set up the most modern leather plant in Dewas that India had ever seen. The moment I saw the factory, I was delighted that it looked just like a subsidiary of TELCO. The factory buildings had high ceilings and were well-engineered. It had a large training school, canteens, homes and everything to make it self-sufficient. It was Moolgaokar's dream come to fruition. Many people from Europe and Russia, with interest in leather, often visited the Dewas Plant.

Even TELCO had been similarly set up in Pune. When TELCO decided to have the plant in Pune, there was a lot of criticism. But the company went on to sow the seeds for the industrialization of Maharashtra in Pune, making the city what it is today. Few people would acknowledge or remember this vital contribution of Moolgaokar, but I certainly do. He did the same thing for Dewas. The decision to put up a leather plant in Dewas was not entirely without controversy. People thought it was far more natural to set it up in Chennai or Kolkata, which were the traditional leather manufacturing centres.

Moolgaokar would recount to me how he would pursue his interest in nature and wildlife photography in the rural areas of Bhopal and Indore when he was younger. He remembered the seven large lakes there. Because he was a naturalist and an environmentalist much before these ideas became popular, and because of his deep love for flora and fauna, the factory in Dewas was as much a beautiful verdant parkland as it was an industrial estate.

One year before the factory was set up, the state government issued TEL with the licence for leather production, on the condition that it would be a 100 per cent export-oriented unit. The plant was established in 1975 as an integrated leather complex and was engaged in manufacturing superior quality finished products—leather shoes, shoe uppers, leather garments and other leather products, primarily for export to Europe and the US. When we started, 95 per cent of the manufactured goods were exported. Gradually, as the government relaxed the norms, the Leather division was also able to sell its products in the domestic market.

On taking charge of TEL, my main task was to turn around the company's business, which had been making losses virtually since its inception. I had to initiate steps to strengthen and expand R&D, upgrade skills and technology, improve quality and productivity, instil financial and management control, do aggressive marketing and formulate plans for its long-term viability and growth. We started updating manufacturing technology to meet the ever-changing requirements of the international market in terms of quality, fashion, delivery and price.

A lot of attention was paid to pollution control and waste water disposal. I was intensely aware of this factory springing up amidst the pristine greenery and being a highly polluting industry, particularly in the small-scale unorganized sector, it had a negative impact on the ecology of the area. However, being part of a large corporate group guided by Moolgaokar's principles, we spared no efforts to make it as clean and pollution-free as possible.

Apart from creating a green environment with many trees, O.K. Kaul, our leather technologist, spent a lot of time in R&D, to develop chemicals for the leather industry and to take care of the effluents from the leather units. After many trials and errors, he came up with a system where not a single drop of water was discharged outside in the drains and nullahs. Our small R&D facility did a fairly good job of manufacturing in-house the chemicals that were required for our tannery and for pollution control. Over a period of time, we further strengthened our R&D lab and aimed to bring the Leather division up to international standards. I am happy that the Tata Leather Finishing Unit set a benchmark for the industry.

The mechanics of leather production fascinated me. I met other private leather tanners and all of them would tell me that the Tatas would never succeed in this business because leather had traditionally been run like a cottage industry on small-scale norms in India. Transactions for buying leather and associated functions were always done in cash. A group like the Tatas, which would only make cheque payments, would thus end up paying a lot more for the same raw materials. We continued to manage the Leather division as a corporation without cutting short on any processes. All the same, I gained some insight and experience into how the industry was regulated and operated.

We reorganized the leather unit by reducing overheads and bringing in job specification. We took a conscious decision to build a strong presence for our leather and leather products divisions in the international markets. Farrokh Kavarana of Tata A.G., Zurich, was helpful. He introduced TEL to Bally Shoes of Switzerland and to many other customers. We started meeting customers abroad to understand their needs so that we could design our goods accordingly. Leather being a fashion product, it was certainly not easy.

As part of our internationalization process, it was essential that we participate in the Paris Leather Show to gain exposure to international markets. TEL's Leather division continued to exhibit footwear, belts and other leather items and participated at the exhibition every year, winning several prizes. I attended the Paris show a couple of times. There were also shows in Bologna in Italy, where leather products from TEL won a lot of applause and recognition. At all the fairs in Italy and France, Tata leather was deemed a premium brand. The division won the award for best performer successively for several years. These were rare honours for India, which was otherwise still struggling in those days to find its footing on the global scenario as a producer of quality leather products. As with any industry hoping to find a place in the international arena, every day was one of improvement to push forward and move ahead.

We had a French consultant, Robert Brouillet, who was a legend in leather tanning and finishing. He was one of the greatest tanners of his time. Like an old-time steelmaker's passion for steel, he had a love for leather. He took up this job as France and Europe had very little leather and related industries left. He stayed alone in Dewas for months trying to help the company become a leading leather unit. He had strong character and displayed tremendous passion for his work and played a significant role in successfully training our young team of professionals to bring them up to international standards. Even during the few months when he was away, visiting his family in Paris, he would be in constant touch with Dewas and receive regular reports and updates. I have known Brouillet for many years and his commitment and passion remained unchanged until he retired at the age of 78.

At Dewas, we had a number of young professionals from IIT besides a few leather technologists and NIFT graduates. I encouraged discussions among them for a common understanding of future development and growth. We reviewed the operations, manufacturing costs, efficiency, market development and achieving greater turnover and higher profits. The Leather Finishing Unit soon began showing definite signs of improvement, achieving 25 per cent higher rate of turnover, better realization, lower rejection and a greater yield. Finally, the division achieved profitability.

Among the professionals, Viren Mehrotra, a topper from IIT, always brought in improvized processes with engineering. He played a key role and at one time was in charge of the whole leather division, which continued to grow progressively. Then there was O.K. Kaul, M.Tech. in leather technology, who worked closely with Brouillet. I once told him to be the 'Brouillet of India'. Kaul went on to become just that. He was recently recognized as one of the world's top 10 tanners.

After his retirement from TEL, Kaul called to tell me that the Indian Leather Council had appointed him chairman of the Committee on Standards for Leather. I was happy to have pushed Kaul and encouraged him to become a top-class tanner. It gave me great satisfaction to know that this man, now past 60, had succeeded in his mission. He earned laurels for the Tatas and for the Indian leather industry. Kaul told me he appreciated the free hand I gave him, allowing him to put his heart and soul into making Dewas the most profitable leather unit of its time in India.

I even got Noel to spend some time in our Dewas leather plant for him to get the feel of the industry. He stayed there for some time and tried to help in retail marketing of leather products. We were also fortunate to have General S.L. Malhotra, whom I met at the Mhow Army headquarters. We requested him to work with us after his retirement and he became general manager of the leather finishing, garment and footwear units. He was a local resident with close connections to the government and the army. Ramesh Subramaniam came from Bata and was earlier the chief for footwear training, UNDP Delhi. He later went on to take charge of our Footwear division in Indore and Chennai. The Leather division had to grapple with many issues, which were effectively resolved by our team of young professionals who did a remarkable job in getting the leather finishing unit to a much higher turnover and profitability. I think the Leather division has done well with the passage of time and made its presence felt globally. We also had strong local impact.

When the land for the leather plant was acquired by TEL, it was all agricultural land and to accommodate the displaced labourers, we offered them jobs in the plant. To transform farm labourers into industrial workers was a big challenge, wherein Kaul played a major role. Consequently, we developed a number of ancillary industries for shoe uppers and other accessories. We also had a footwear division run by girls who were more dexterous and nimble with their hands. They were all above 18 years and locally employed and constituted the women workforce of the Footwear division. Ultimately, teamwork paid off. We exported to countries worldwide, including China.

I continued to instil in the team the need to adapt to new technology, stay relevant in the field and to be aware of competition. Technology upgradation was important, though one had to also train people in finance, planning and operations. While meeting various departments of the leather unit in Dewas, we would go through the annual plan. I always requested the Planning Department to play a role in broadening departmental activities and also to look out for markets in which they could expand and develop new products. My trips to Dewas were usually over an extended period and always enjoyable. In the evenings, Viren and his wife Mamta, would organize enjoyable get-togethers. Today as I look back, I wish to acknowledge the contributions made by each person in our dedicated team. The team members worked together to achieve the highest standards. They could have gone anywhere in the world, but chose to stay in Dewas, which offered little by way of good schools or colleges and their wives could not get a job of their choice. Yet, they persisted because they wanted to meet the challenge head on and because they sought to match our production standards to those of the Italians, who were one of the main players in the world for leather and fashion goods. I salute all of them today. TEL's Leather division is a great holistic success story.

I am reminded of the moment when I thanked Moolgaokar for all his support in promoting high-tech new businesses under TEL and he simply responded by saying that he never invested in projects, but in the person behind these projects. These words of encouragement are worth a trillion bucks!

Overseas Expansion

TEL initially had a few offices abroad, one of which was in Berlin. Thereafter, we developed many other representative offices worldwide. TEL set up offices in Cyprus, Bangladesh, Russia and the UK. We even posted a man in London in the office of Tata Ltd so that we could explore the market in Europe for our shoe and leather products.

Ratan once called and introduced me to the chairman of Jebel Ali Free Trade Zone in Dubai. The chairman explained the various exciting opportunities to work in Dubai where there are no taxes in the free trade zone. Based on the various considerations, we decided to explore the opportunity and finally set up a base in Jebel Ali Free Trade Zone in the late 1980s. The operations were successful.

I thought we should review our offices and concentrate on the ones which offered future business possibilities like Hong Kong. In the 1980s, I realized that Hong Kong would be future destination although we opened the first office there in 1994 to cater to the Chinese market and to understand how they functioned. It would open up business opportunities by getting to know people on either side. This office also served as an effective entry port for TCS and Tata Steel to start their operations in this region.

There was never a dull moment working in TEL. We needed to be constantly aware and alive to the industrial and export-import policies of the government, which were ever-changing. At the same time, we also provide the government feedback and suggestions on trade policies —which were bearing positive results—and those that could be looked into for improvement of the economy.

As part of the Tata Group globalization plan, we studied various markets and finally zeroed in on Africa as a continent for the future. Tata Zambia was already established in 1978 as a 100 per cent subsidiary of TEL, before I took over as MD of TEL. We were driven by the idea of expansion. Our motto was: 'Expansion through marketing and distribution channel of your products'. This export business was done with great passion and pride. The margins were thin and the stakes high, but long-term relationships emerged as the clear winner as we shall see in the next chapter.

Chapter 6

THE AFRICA STORY

Jawaharlal Nehru had said that the Independence of India was incomplete without that of African nations. The freedom struggle that swept across Africa in the 1960–70s gave the continent a number of heroes. These leaders, who drew inspiration from India's struggle for freedom, held high positions in various governments in later years. The wave of political liberation sweeping across the African continent, was quickly followed by a rising demand for infrastructure and logistics handling by the governments. The newly formed governments, albeit at different paces, were tackling restrictive laws and opening up their economies and actively encouraging foreign investments. The strong India-Africa linkages made for a solid canvass against which business opportunities could be explored.

A bright and vibrant land with 300 days of sunshine and a greater landmass than India, Africa offered attractive opportunities for new businesses. It has always been endowed with vast natural resources, so the opportunities in agriculture, horticulture, mining, transport, power and tourism were attractive as they potentially had high returns on investment. I found out from the records that a high-level team led by Saklatvala, managing director of Tata Limited, London, had visited Africa in the year 1975 to explore business opportunities. Zambia, at the time, was politically stable and although the economy was largely state-owned, the country was fertile for the exploration of business opportunities.

At Home in Zambia

The Tata Group had a bold vision for growth and a long-term strategy for Africa as early as 1977, when we first forayed into Zambia. The establishment of Tata Zambia Limited (TZL) as a wholly owned subsidiary of TEL in October of that year signalled the Group's entry into the African market. The primary objective of TZL was to promote exports of Tata vehicles, agricultural machinery and implements, including tractors and sprinklers. Looking beyond what Zambia had to offer, Africa proved to be a land of opportunities for those with a long-term business view. Tata Zambia was the ideal springboard to expand the Tatas' operations in sub-Saharan Africa and other Central African countries to increase our business reach in international trade as well as expose our people to the competition abroad. Looking back on our journey, we eventually reached out to 22 African countries. The Africa story is a tribute to the bond I share with the people in many nations of this diverse continent.

Africa occupied a special place in my life. Sometime in the mid-1960s, during my early days in Jamshedpur, Ratan had informally told me that Africa has huge potential and opportunities, and that we should seriously consider doing some pioneering work in the continent. We were both fairly young then and neither of us had set foot on this vast continent before. However, this conversation with Ratan remained with me. My first opportunity to take a close look at Africa came when I returned from Singapore to Mumbai as managing director of TEL.

I shall always remember my first visit to Zambia in 1983. This was to act as a primer, to familiarize myself with our operations in Lusaka, Zambia's capital. This visit was vital as it helped me get acquainted with their government and dignitaries besides developing a future plan of action for Tata Zambia to become a prominent organization in that region.

I flew the Zambian Airways from Mumbai and arrived on a bright sunny morning in Lusaka's small, clean and friendly airport. While driving to Pamodzi Hotel, I saw vast expanses of greenery with well laid out roads lined by tall trees. Jacarandas bloomed everywhere. There were few people on the roads. I realized at once that Zambia was a beautiful country, blessed by nature with an abundance of flora and fauna. The weather was excellent and people on the streets looked content, healthy and happy.

In a strange way, I felt a sense of déjà-vu and completely at home here in this unknown land! It reminded me of Jamshedpur. Within hours, I was committed to explore possibilities in Africa. Zambia was politically stable then as it is now. The country had gained Independence in 1964 and the economy was heavily controlled in the 1970s with a conglomeration of state-owned entities. Zambian mines were the second highest producers of copper in the world and the economy, though dependent on export of copper and other minerals, was doing well. The currency, Kwacha, was stronger than the US dollar.

We were running our operation in Zambia from our centrally located office on Cha-Cha Road in the city, where I met all our managers and staff members. Raman Dhawan, a bright chartered accountant, was one of the younger managers there and had just taken over as the head of Zambia operations. My other staff members were from TELCO because our business was focused on marketing commercial vehicles and doing engineering jobs. At that time, one in three commercial vehicles in Zambia was a Tata vehicle.

Building Relationships

Anil K. Sethi was in charge of Makumbi Agricultural and Tractor Company (MATCO), a wholly owned subsidiary of Tata Zambia. MATCO was a small company manufacturing agricultural machinery and products. I walked around our warehouse and was briefed about our operations. During my discussion with our colleagues in Tata Zambia, I said, 'We have to do something worthwhile here, as it appears there are plenty of opportunities.' I was however, informed about a rather worrying trend when I wanted to meet key government officials—an attitude of indifference by important authorities in the country towards us. We tried to meet several ministers, as was the conventional practice, but sensed resistance as they were not inclined to meet us. There was a general sentiment that the Tatas had come in with a lot of promises, but had not delivered.

When Sethi arranged my meeting with the Minister of Agriculture, we were made to wait for a long time and I could sense that our presence was generally not accepted, appreciated or welcomed. Finally, the meeting took place, seemingly with much reluctance on his part. We brought forward most of the conflicting issues in terms of growth and expansion of the business and recommended a mutually amicable way out to overcome these problems. Gradually, the discussions turned more positive. I assured the minister that while there was a change in management at TEL, our policies and commitment remained unchanged and I would personally take steps to improve our engagement with Zambia. This interaction turned out to be fruitful and marked the positive start of a long journey.

Our next priority was to meet relevant officials in the Ministry of Power and Minerals. Once again, we faced the same reluctance and resistance and encountered the usual delay. We provided them the necessary assurances to respond to their request for power plant machinery.

We even tried to meet the then president of Zambia, His Excellency Kenneth Kaunda, as was the usual protocol for any visiting executive or delegation from an overseas organization. Getting this appointment too, was difficult. However, with the kind intervention of the then Indian Deputy High Commissioner, Shiv Mukherjee, we finally met the President at the Presidential Palace in Lusaka, over a dinner meeting.

We went into the meeting well prepared, as we knew it was going to be a tough interaction. However, the president turned out to be an affable person and received us warmly. He discreetly conveyed to us that Tatas had not lived up to their promises. He mentioned that the Tatas could have taken advantage of the opportunities that existed and offered to them in Zambia by taking up the businesses abandoned and sold off by Europeans after Zambia's Independence from the British.

I could sense the President's disappointment as well as his concern, but neither did he elaborate nor speak further on the matter. I explained to him our future plan: how we intended to make Zambia our base and to reach out to the rest of Africa. I tried to convince the president that TEL would do everything possible to win back his confidence. I added that we had the full support of our top management and that we would cooperate and work hard with the government in Zambia. He was, however, not convinced and remained non-committal.

As we were leaving, President Kaunda said to me, 'Gupta, I heard what you had to say. I will be happy to give you a chance to expand your business in Zambia.'

This meeting laid the foundation for a long and special relationship that we were to shape and share in the future, culminating in President Kaunda appointing me as the Honorary

Consul General for the Republic of Zambia in Mumbai in July 1987. The appointment was signed by President Kaunda and as the first Honorary Consul for Zambia, my role was to promote Indian investments in Zambia and increase bilateral trade and promote tourism.

Coming back to our initial days, my visit to Zambia till now had been far from fruitful. The reception had been lukewarm. The Zambian government had made it abundantly clear that they had no faith in the Tatas or India, and did not look upon us as serious business partners. It was exasperating. Yet, although I had returned from our first meeting with the president, disappointed and dejected, I was not discouraged or disheartened. It strengthened my resolve to build a strong base in Zambia for the Tata Group and improve relations between the two countries. I wanted to cement our ties strongly so that the Tata Story in Africa would be a torch-bearer for many others to follow. Our team got down to reviewing the meeting with the president. It appeared that in spite of our best intentions, our hands were tied. What was promised to Zambia in terms of investments and projects was delayed primarily due to the restrictive economic policies prevailing in India at the time, especially our stringent foreign exchange regulations. Yet, no information about these delays was provided to the Zambian government. We thus had a strained relationship with Zambia due to these lapses and also a gap in communication on our part. I told the team we had to do everything to reverse the situation for the future. We had to rebuild a good working relationship based on trust in order to do business in this country.

The meeting with President Kaunda played a pivotal role in the way we structured our business plans thereafter for Zambia. It had a bearing on the type of businesses we were to do in the country and the strategy we formulated for geographic expansion in the region and outside it.

Our initial task was to target the immediate needs of the country. We began to look for opportunities to align ourselves with the government's socio-economic objectives to create employment opportunities for the people of Zambia. We reached out our intention to the Zambian government.

Soon after our preliminary meetings, the government approached us to take over and manage Luangwa Industries, one of the state-owned bicycle manufacturing entities being managed by Industrial Development Corporation (INDECO) Limited, a government-owned organization, at Chipata. It was both a surprise and a great honour for us to be considered as the first choice by the president himself.

In the early 1980s, although the Zambian economy was stable, there were signs of financial weakness in certain business sectors, which were steadily deepening into a financial crisis. There was a large number of sick public-sector companies that needed to be revived. In response to the crisis, the government took the decision to offer management contracts of several state-owned enterprises to private-sector companies. TZL took over the management contract of Luangwa Bicycle Industries.

It was a difficult project. The manufacturing base was located in Chipata, a long distance from Lusaka, which offered market for bicycles. Logistics were a real challenge and the finished goods had to travel long distances to reach the markets. By reworking the logistics, TEL managed to reduce costs. Within the first two years of our takeover, this previously unviable unit started generating profits.

This was an important turnaround for us as it enhanced our image as a successful business house in Zambia. The Tatas always took pride in partnering with governments in improving the lives of people. Bicycles provided an economical means of transport when oil prices were steadily climbing. TZL operated within the parameters of the management contract for a decade, from 1987 to 1997, before it acquired Luangwa Industries in totality.

The Zambian government also told us about a shoe factory in the plant that made shoes for the army, but was not performing well. We helped them by sending in our experts, but did not take over the management of the plant.

By the late 1980s, we saw a marked improvement in our relations with Zambia and arranged for a visit by Palkhivala. In a meeting with President Kaunda, issues like health, nutrition and creation of jobs in Zambia were duly discussed.

However, the TEL chairman could perceive that severe malnutrition and undernourishment among the population was a serious concern. It was especially worrisome that the Zambian people's diet was severely deficient in protein. At that time, proteins in the form of meat and poultry were to a large extent the preserve of a privileged few. Not everyone could afford to eat meat on a regular basis. The staple diet of majority of the population consisted of ground maize, which was usually eaten as porridge, accompanied by some vegetables like spinach or beans. This protein deficiency was not as prevalent among Zambia's neighbouring countries that had access to fish through community fishing. Although Zambia was a landlocked country with no affordable access to a coastline, it was blessed with large lakes. Thus, when the President requested our help in setting up fish farming, we readily agreed to take up this challenge.

I knew Dr M. Sinha, the director at Central Inland Fishery Research Institute in India. He identified Brajendra Kumar, who had a master's degree in Fishery, as our possible guide in sustainable fish farming. We inducted him in TEL and briefed him on TZL. Subsequently, he was posted in Zambia for about two years and did a very good job in this joint venture between TZL and Zambia Consolidated Copper Mines (ZCCM). Fish farms set up at various sites generated employment for the surrounding communities. We drew from resources within the country using an indigenous species of fish, the Tilapia, to provide protein and nourishment for the majority of the population. The people of Zambia now had a new source of protein to choose from and a more balanced diet. Tata showed its commitment to the country and Zambian society.

Promoting Business, Breakthroughs and the Tata Name

In the mornings when I jogged around Lusaka with Raman, I really enjoyed the feel of the city. It had character and colour and was quite a prosperous capital. I was pleased to see a lot of international names and foreign branded products. Later, I met some executives from other commercial organizations operating in Lusaka. They were basically representing various manufacturers of plant and equipment in Europe and marketing them in Zambia and its neighbouring countries.

While on the road, I noticed portable gensets, crushers, road rollers and concrete mixers mostly from European countries being used in Zambia. There was no Indian equipment visible. People in Zambia and other African countries relied only on machines from Europe. The products were all specified by the Europeans and US manufacturers and this had worked for them historically. They just did not believe that India had a good manufacturing base for trucks, trains, power plants and construction machineries or infrastructure equipment.

Unlike Indian teachers, doctors and researchers, who were well respected, most Africans, since colonial times, largely looked upon the community of Indian businessmen as basically traders; who did their business in Africa and lived in London while their heart was in India. Hence, as far as India was concerned, the attitude of the disbelieving Africans was 'seeing is believing.' This was the gap we needed to address. Our task, to change this mindset, was a major challenge. However, we were gradually able to show that the performance of our trucks was at par with other international competitors. In fact, getting our trucks on their roads played a major role in improving India's image along with that of Tatas'.

We needed to meet the relevant people and make them aware that India could compete well with Europeans in many fields. This was true not only for Zambia but also other African countries as they were simply not exposed to Indian manufacturers. This was a challenging task for TZL.

We invited relevant organizations in Zambia and later on, from other African countries to visit us in India to get first-hand knowledge about our capabilities. We also put the initiative through CII and other trade bodies in India requesting them to make an effort to expose key enterprises to our manufacturing capabilities in India. Here, I must mention that CII, Exim bank and the Ministry of Commerce played a major role in exposing African countries to our manufacturing capabilities. It is different now, with most of our products and services well accepted in Africa.

Although I had international experience, the challenges associated with African markets were significantly different from the ones in Europe where you were judged by the quality of your technical expertise. The majority of our staff in Zambia was unaware about the Group's activities and the business culture. I could see that individuals in each department worked in isolation and therefore a reorientation of the staff was necessary to promote the Group and the Tata brand name with a view to generate global business. Malgham of TEL, Mumbai, and I, therefore, set out a plan to familiarize these employees with the Tata Group for its activities, culture and philanthropy.

We also worked to identify new business areas. During discussions with my colleagues, it became clear that we should initially focus on three primary sectors—mining, hospitality and transportation. Zambia is blessed with a lot of fertile land, water and minerals. We had to enter the mining business for which we need not own mines, but could provide mining support services. The Tata Group had expertise in mining and could always draw on this know-how to get into mining and allied services in Africa. This turned out to be a breakthrough decision.

I instinctively felt the need to venture into the hospitality sector in Zambia. The hotel where I was staying, Pamodzi, was part of the state-owned National Hotels Group in Zambia. With the spurt in tourism, I could sense collaborative possibilities for Pamodzi with Indian hotels. I felt we could consider taking it over to make a mark in the hospitality industry in Africa. Even this decision worked out well. We also needed to intensify our presence in the transportation sector. Although, doing well in vehicles trade, we needed to provide long-term support to the customer.

This was the brief I gave my team in 1983. I also told my colleagues that as they lived in Zambia and dealt with the people and government, they should come up with business or project ideas, which will be more relevant. Further, if they had any fresh suggestions or ideas, they should discuss among themselves and write to us at the Head Office. My first visit to Zambia thus left an indelible mark in my life.

On my return to India, I called a meeting of all concerned managers to brief them on the approach to explore the many business opportunities available in Africa. Mr Hoshie Malgham was appointed to take charge of corporate affairs. Later on an Africa Desk was created and Amrita Banerjee, an executive in the Corporate Office was appointed to liaise with the operating departments and African businesses. We started chalking out plans for Zambia and how we could best approach Africa. We needed to create two separate verticals—mining and hospitality—and also bring in the right people. These African projects were supported by relevant divisions set up at Tata Exports in India. It was quite an exciting period in the company and for me personally. However, conditions in pre-liberalized India before 1991 remained challenging and coloured most of our business decisions.

Credibility Challenge

Exporting of goods was difficult with a laborious process of filling up a multitude of forms. Foreign exchange allowances were low. Anyone travelling abroad had to apply for permission from the Indian government and the Reserve Bank of India, enclosing a letter of invitation from parties abroad, list of meetings scheduled and other relevant details. For instance, when Dhawan was deputed to Zambia, he had to leave within a week of his appointment or be classified as an Indian Resident. He left with his wife and infant with an allowance of US$20—$8 each for him and his wife, and $4 for the baby. Today, things have changed for the better.

Communication too, was primitive and slow. We could only rely on the post and booking of trunk calls, which was expensive. There was no direct dialling service. Eventually, technology changed with the arrival of telex service. This was a huge boon for exporters and enabled us to work a lot more efficiently.

Once, we had an absolutely shocking experience in Zambia and were saved by the telex. It was in the mid-1980s. One of our staff discovered bricks in cartons, which were supposed to contain spare parts. The bricks had obviously come from India, as these were made of clay and different from the ones in Zambia, which were made of concrete blocks. This needed immediate investigation. As it is, people and goods from India were viewed with suspicion, and this incident could prove a further setback for our credibility. Some Indian transporters had obviously broken the law, and it was not the Tatas.

During the investigation, we found that a special spare part called 'crown wheel pinion' was in short supply in India. The truckers knew from the list of contents in transit, what part was packed where for export, and at some point, removed the pinions and replaced them with bricks with equal weight. Thanks to telex, being the only written proof (as opposed to calls which were not recorded), we managed to prove our innocence in the incident. Following our report on the wrong-doing, another agency too reported a similar experience. Ultimately, the racket was busted by government agencies.

I had gained vast knowledge with my business experience in Singapore, where we faced warlike situations every day to market India and the Tata brand. Singapore had taught me a lot about customer relationships. In Zambia, however, it was a different battle altogether. Unlike Singapore with an open market, Zambia and Africa were closed markets and licences were necessary for import and export of goods.

We were selling trucks that had a long life span. So, buyers would be married to the vehicle for the next 25 years. Our challenge was to convince potential buyers to take on an expensive long-term product without being an internationally known brand.

In those days, the purchase meant a substantial principal investment and maintenance cost of the vehicle. The buyer had to come up with the entire money as there were no banking facilities such as loans. We, therefore, had to provide lease financing to increase our sales. To do this, we arranged a line of credit for the buyer from EXIM Bank. Our next hurdle was to provide long-term support to the customer in terms of spare parts and service as spares were in short supply. It was an uphill task that needed a lot of perseverance.

To have our trucks or any parts approved for quality control in Zambia was a problem. Specifications were drawn up by Europeans and to get approval from the authorities took a long time. We had to constantly prove that our trucks were as good as other international brands even though they were cheaper in price. It took time, but we met the authorities and urged them to test our trucks and compare them with international brands. Eventually, TEL took over all the dealerships of Tata Motors and made it a successful business.

Spare parts, however, continued to plague us. If there were accidents, spares were not readily available. Tata trucks used original spares which were invariably in short supply. It was, therefore, soon mandated that Tata Motors must produce enough spares to cater to export markets. One day's total production had to be kept in reserve both in India and abroad. There were times when we bought spare parts from Indian markets and shipped them to Africa, as the worst thing that could happen to us at this stage was not to have a Tata truck running on the road due to lack of spares. We had to meet customer expectations. We gradually improved our performance by training our people to handle customers, opening a customer service centre and building a large warehouse to store spares.

Despite various challenges, we never gave up. Soon, Tata trucks were a great success and we branched from Zambia to other countries like Tanzania, Kenya and Ghana. Soon after South Africa held its first elections, we took our business there too. My colleagues in Africa did a great job setting up the extensive network for marketing Tata vehicles. In the end, it was primarily a trust-building exercise. We could move forward because customers, and eventually, the society, began to rely on us.

Spirit of Entrepreneurship

The Tata Zambia team in Africa was highly motivated with a pioneering spirit under the dynamic leadership of Raman Dhawan. He built up the team with specialized product knowledge and also developed relationship in African countries at the highest levels. We wanted to be part of the development of the Zambian and other African economies. For the Tatas, Africa was not the 'Dark Continent' as known in the world, but a diamond in the rough. And Zambia was our first post. The country offered many exciting opportunities in several fields with its huge land mass, small population size and great bio-diversity.

Mining Machines: The Zambian economy was historically dependent on copper mining. However, all mining equipment and spares was imported and the Germans, British and the Americans controlled the industry tightly. The Zambians were never given the drawings to make spares and were left with no alternative, but to depend on the West for all their equipment and spares, which were sold at high prices.

We immediately saw an opportunity in this industry. We offered to make mining spares and equipment for them at a much more reasonable price. TEL created a small engineering department in Kolkata where we re-engineered spare parts that were required in Zambia and started exporting them. While developing the business, we took help from Tata Steel. It was an interesting process, which we enjoyed doing and it became a viable business proposition for us; especially when Zambian Copper Mines appointed TZL as its procurement agent for spare parts from India.

We continue our involvement to this day by supplying a number of mining products including valves, bearings, rubber linings, graphite electrodes, as used in cobalt processing and seals. Steel, mainly steel plates, were supplied to the local market and tyres were sourced from India.

Pamodzi Hospitality: When I first arrived in Lusaka, the country was seeing a spurt in tourism and the state-owned National Hotels wanted to offer a management contract to private parties for operating Hotel Pamodzi. Both the Taj and the Oberoi were shortlisted for this partnership. However, not wanting to lose this opportunity of entering the hospitality sector in Zambia, we coordinated the India visit with officials of National Hotels and successfully convinced them to give the Taj Group the contract for running the hotel for 10 years, in 1990.

In later years, TZL bid for acquiring the full equity of Pamodzi Hotel and secured a 70 per cent stake. The hotel came under the Taj Hotels and Resorts umbrella. It has undergone significant refurbishment to ensure that standards are met and brand consistency maintained.

Once, Ratan, while on a visit to South Africa in October 2004, visited Zambia and was given a rousing welcome at the airport with a motorcade. He was received by top government officials before proceeding to the hotel. Ratan stayed at the Taj Pamodzi Hotel and was impressed by the services offered. He also made some suggestions to further improve the standards of the hotel, which were duly implemented. Late President Levy Mwanawasa—who was in power from January 2002 until his death in August 2008—inaugurated the new-look Taj Pamodzi during his presidency. President Mwanawasa also hosted a dinner at the Presidential Palace for Ratan, where he had the opportunity to meet Zambian ministers and bureaucrats. The president discussed with him many business opportunities and promised all help for future development, growth and training plans.

Promoting Agriculture: Copper was responsible for around 90 per cent of Zambia's foreign exchange earnings. Its prices collapsed in the late 1970s causing alarm and forced the government to look at other alternatives. Zambia had fertile rain-fed lands, which were ideal for commercial farming. Traditional crops included tobacco, maize, sugar and cotton.

In the early 1980s, TZL acquired a large landholding in an attempt to grow energy-based products like rapeseed, which produce bio-fuel. However, this did not happen as we had envisaged and the project was not successful. The land was converted for agricultural purposes. Later, I visited one of the largest farms in Zambia owned by a gentleman called Galun. He owned vast tracts of land and was a large employer in the region, producing cereals and vegetables for local production as well as for export, which sparked another project. TEL bought a piece of land near his farm at a reasonable price and started vegetable farming with two planters from Kerala. We cultivated okra and other vegetables in Zambia.

The country's location and climate made it an ideal place for floriculture. So we set up a rose farm just outside Lusaka with Dutch expertise. We established Tata Farms and Foods and this TZL subsidiary raised field crops such as maize, wheat, vegetables and roses on a 500-hectare plot in Ngwerere, near Lusaka. The produce went beyond local consumption and we started exporting long-stem roses to Holland and the UK. This created employment and in keeping with the Tata philosophy of community development, we also set up a school near its operations.

We always felt the need to develop the skills of the local people who could then contribute more effectively and be an integral part of their development and subsequently of the business. Schools were set up to train selected local technicians, some of whom were sent to India to work at the Tata Motors plants for advanced training. This was reassuring for the customers and empowering for the technicians.

Subsequently, due to inadequacy of communication and flight connections between Lusaka and Europe, the activity became unviable over the years and we leased out the farm where business was continued with the same staff at the time. Even the school was handed over to a new business party.

Powering Zambia: We also ventured into power generation by setting up a 120-MW ITT hydropower station located in Southern

Province. It was a joint venture between TZL and Zambia Electric Supply Corporation (ZESCO). Built at a cost of $245 million on the Kafue River, some 300 km from the confluence of the Kafue and Zambezi rivers, the Kafue Hydropower Station was originally constructed to provide storage capacity for the Kafue Gorge Power Station, with both ITPC and ZESCO operating the Itezhi-Tezhi Dam as a shared facility.

Healing Medicines: There was a great demand for pharmaceutical products in Zambia. However, the prices were high as these products were mostly imported from Europe. The President believed this was an opportunity to be exploited to Zambia's advantage. Importing generic medicines from India would give access to affordable medicines to the people of Zambia. TZL thus imported generics from India and handled the marketing and distribution.

Zambia and its wonderful people will always hold a special place in my heart. I share many fond memories of my experiences in the country and the friendly, hospitable and hardworking people. I have always tried to promote Africa-India relationship rather than pure commerce for which I often faced some criticism. One person, however, who always stood by me, was Ratan. He told me once, 'Syamal, we are remembered in Africa because of what we did there in setting up a space for an industrial base for the country to build on, through training and development. If we went only for business, we would never have developed this long-term relationship.' This was reassuring to me.

Ratan always had a keen interest in Zambia and visited various TZL departments and workshops. He encouraged the marketing departments to aggressively push products and services of the highest quality. He met our staff and discussed future growth strategy and was happy with their performance.

In fact, during my association of over 17 years, we made every effort to train and develop good managers from existing staff member of TZL. This was the time in the 1980s when no other Indian company would go to Africa and there was a dearth of trained talent. There were quite a few who shaped up well with the training. One of them was Dhawan—who proved to be a very successful executive of TZL. He was honest, hardworking and sincere and worked closely with the head office for further growth and development of the various businesses. Later, he was appointed managing director of all Tata operations in South Africa in recognition of his significant contribution.

Zambia was my learning turf in Africa about working in an entirely different culture. This is where we developed our connections to the continent as well. I realized Africa relied on the UK the same way India had relied on it in the past. Zambians too visited the UK frequently. Our meeting ground for business development was the Commonwealth Business Council and the School of Oriental and African Studies, much visited by businesspersons and government officials alike. When we meet outside our own countries, it is a level playing field.

India played an important role in the economic and technological revival of the Zambian economy. Today, Zambia has matured as a democracy and is a strong country with vast resources. I see it growing in strength as a role model for emerging democracies. It is the strong relationships we developed in Zambia that has resulted in Tata Group being one of the biggest investors in Africa today. The beneficial bilateral relations between India and Zambia paved the way for our pioneering foray into other African countries as well.

Journey through Africa

Having established our brand in Zambia, TEL started looking around the surrounding markets in southern Africa to set up subsidiaries primarily for marketing and servicing of Tata commercial vehicles.

Our philosophy of putting community development at the centre of business strategy came to be known as the 'Zambia Model' and this was replicated in other African countries like Zimbabwe, Namibia, Tanzania, Mozambique, Uganda, Ghana, Kenya and Nigeria with varying results. Our most notable impact was in South Africa.

South Africa: As the most developed economy in the continent, South Africa had a stable financial sector. In 1994, when South Africa held its first universal elections, it was a watershed year for its people, and the world and the Tatas celebrated their political achievement.

Soon thereafter, in 1996, Thabo Mbeki, deputy president of South Africa visited Mumbai. Their Consul General, Jacques De Vos, organized meetings with several Indian industries in Mumbai. We had an opportunity to meet the deputy president and make a presentation on the Tatas. He was impressed with the Group and mentioned that he would like the Tatas to come to South Africa for business.

We felt that besides being welcomed, there were good business opportunities in South Africa, which would be mutually beneficial. As the largest African economy, South Africa had around 45 million consumers at that time. The industrial infrastructure could match that of any developed country and it had an efficient port, and sophisticated financial, business and commercial services environment embedded in an export-oriented environment.

When we briefed Ratan on our discussion with Thabo Mbeki, and the possibilities in South Africa, he encouraged us to look at the country closely. We continued our discussion through Dhawan about opening up business in South Africa.

South Africa seemed like a natural launching pad for doing business in the rest of Africa and the decision to shift the corporate base from Zambia to South Africa was an informed choice. In fact, soon after Tata Africa Holdings, South Africa, was founded in 1994, the expansion into sub-Saharan Africa was put in place.

However, when we first arrived in South Africa, we had to contend with a saturated market within which we needed to carve out a niche offering just to survive. This was a challenge. Our traditional route for entry into other African nations had been our commercial vehicles, but here in South Africa, the market was not going to be receptive to this approach. We had to first identify several priority sectors which were underserved or untapped. We then leveraged the Group's strength to address this issue. The priority sectors we focused on were power, telecommunications, steel, mining, hospitality, consulting and, to some extent, pharmaceuticals.

Neotel, South Africa's second largest fixed line operator was a subsidiary of Tata Communications. Tata Motors started as a distribution centre for passenger and commercial vehicles in South Africa, and expanded into building bus body in 2004 in Pretoria.

Taj International Hotels (SA) Pty Ltd was formed in 2006 as a subsidiary and a joint venture between The Indian Hotels Company and Tata Africa Holdings, to offer 5-star luxury of the legendary Taj standards. Today, Taj Cape Town complements Taj Pamodzi, and the two properties reflect the Tatas' commitment to the hospitality industry.

TCS offers IT consultancy services in South Africa for government and business clients and has often used this as a base to expand into the region and also enlarge the scope of services. The Group companies have also got local partnerships as part of the Black Economic Empowerment programme of the government. The Tatas' move to partner with South Africa was, therefore, an important link in the Group's internationalization.

Thabo Mbeki, then president of South Africa, included Ratan in his Presidential Business Advisory Board, which had several high-profile government officials and international industrialists.

Ratan was also appointed the first co-chairman of the India-Africa CEOs Forum, along with Patrice Motsepe, who represented South Africa. The first meeting of this Forum was held in Johannesburg. A high-profile body, it was formed with the support of both the governments; and annual meetings are held every alternate year in the two countries to promote business and develop cultural relations.

Ratan had to visit South Africa regularly to attend high-profile meetings. During these visits, he would review all Tata business operations. He would always spend valuable time to meet and discuss the marketing of Tata vehicles, besides the products and services of other joint ventures with our respective business executives and agencies to ensure qualitative products were offered to the South African public. He would also visit the 'ZeroTec' vehicle testing facility set up by the South African government for testing all vehicles sold in the country, to see the performance of various brands.

Social Development: Zanele Mbeki, the former First Lady of South Africa and chairperson of Women's Development Banking Trust, had a keen interest in the social and economic development of the underprivileged. She sought cooperation from the Tatas in several projects related to the welfare and training of women and children. Madame Mbeki closely observed some key welfare and training centres in Kolkata and Jamshedpur and was impressed by the range of activities undertaken in the areas of education, health, sanitation and adult literacy.

Soon thereafter, the Tatas appointed teams to South Africa to identify areas of cooperation and to initiate employment-generating programmes aimed at women's empowerment and training in the field of goat farming, leather tanning, craft, ceramics and jewellery design.

TCS also assisted with the development of an appropriate module for the rural poor, when a pilot project was initiated towards adult literacy along the lines of a successful experiment in India.

The pilot project was in Pedi language, a dialect in northern Sotho, one of the 11 official South African languages.

Zimbabwe: We entered Zimbabwe, Zambia's neighbouring country, in the late 1980s. Zimbabwe had just emerged from a civil war with the white colonizers of the Republic of Southern Rhodesia. Also, in 1982, with the removal of sanctions imposed on it by the United Nations, this nation seemed to offer the most potential. The land was rich in minerals and could be successfully cultivated. It was also the most industrialized country in the continent after South Africa. However, events in the country in later years did not offer us the same level of success as we had achieved in Zambia.

In 1983, we decided to set up a wholly owned subsidiary in Zimbabwe. The country's ruling white elite still controlled much of the economy and TEL was the first business group from a non-white country intending to set up base there. We could however, feel the strong resistance as the bureaucracy tried to ensure the Tatas did not get permission. It took us a long time before we could start our activity of marketing and servicing Tata vehicles. We did not, however, stop at this and soon started to sell other products, notably bicycles and pharmaceuticals.

However, Zimbabwe, which had started out with so much hope went into a downward spiral because of political reasons. The government's move to control tobacco and cotton plantations led to widespread arson, internal strife and insecurity, which badly affected its economy. In that situation, Tata Zimbabwe had become virtually dormant and considered unviable until, a few years later, it was revived to a certain extent in the late 1990s and continues to do business today.

Tanzania: This country has always shared a special relationship with India. Former President Julius Nyerere was held in high esteem in India and was conferred the Jawaharlal Nehru Award for

International Understanding in 1974 and the International Gandhi Peace Prize in 1995.

We set up Tata Holdings (Tanzania) in 1994 for general trade of engineering goods, chemicals, bearings and construction glass. Later, a bicycle manufacturing unit was also set up in the country in association with a Zambian company. We cast this net in Dar-es-Salaam as the entry port for a larger share in East Africa. We did not venture into Tanzania with vehicles as Tata Motors had already made inroads into the market. Our main strategy was to capitalize on the country's strategic location to establish trade extending to Rwanda, Burundi, Malawi and parts of the Democratic Republic of Congo, which were all heavily dependent on Tanzania for their imports. Passenger vehicles were well perceived by the middle class there as they were seen as modern and affordable.

I was appointed as a member of the International Investors' Round Table Conference set up by the World Bank and the International Monetary Fund in 2003. The president of Tanzania chaired these meetings for discussion on national issues for industry and trade.

Kenya: Within the East Africa hub, Tata Africa, Kenya, was set up in 2005 with offices in Nairobi. As with most other African nations, we once again rode on the back of Tata Motors, but quickly expanded to include information and communication technology and pharmaceuticals, thus opening up opportunities for further expansion and exploration of other business areas.

Nigeria: As with most African countries, commercial vehicles proved to be the winner in Nigeria too, which we entered with in 2006. Nigeria was then the second-largest economy in sub-Saharan Africa and the most populated in the continent, and therefore, a major market for us.

The country had a healthy demand for used vehicles, including Tata trucks due to the strict import policies and gradually this market developed an appetite. Demand, therefore, grew for new passenger vehicles. In response, we decided to form Tata Africa, Nigeria Services, with a showroom and appointed dealers for our vehicles.

Mozambique: Our foray into Mozambique was to pursue opportunities in coal and agriculture. Tata Holdings, Mozambique, represents Tata Africa through two offices. The then president of the Republic of Mozambique, Joaquim Alberto Chissano, visited the TEL office in May 2003 accompanied by his ministers and senior government officials. We were keen to explore prospects in mini-hydel power plants, salt, water conservation, construction, material handling equipment, transport and IT-enabled literacy programmes. Subsequently, there were delegations from Mozambique visiting India, which we hosted.

Today, our endeavour to develop relationship with various African governments and industry to promote business has paid off. Tata Africa is on an aggressive growth path and has a good team in place with excellent industry and government connections. It has seen unprecedented success and is poised for exponential growth on the back of global demand for oil, minerals and food. We had seen its early potential and I am happy that we had aligned our growth plans with that of the African continent to be amongst the top 50 businesses in Africa.

The Tatas has operated its various businesses from South Africa, Zambia, Namibia, Zimbabwe, Tanzania, Kenya, Nigeria, Senegal, Congo, Rwanda, Burundi, Malawi, Mozambique and Ghana over the years.

By 2000, TEL had 10 overseas subsidiaries—Tata Africa Holdings (SA) (Pty) Limited in South Africa, Tata Zambia Limited in Zambia, Tata Ghana Limited in Ghana, Tata Uganda Limited in

Uganda, Tata Namibia (Pty) Limited in Namibia, Tata Zimbabwe (Pty) Limited in Zimbabwe, Tata Holdings (Tanzania) Limited in Tanzania, and Tata Holdings Mozambique Limited in Mozambique in addition to Tata South-East Asia Limited (TSEA) in Hong Kong and Tata (UAE) FZE in Dubai. TEL also has an office in Thailand and has participated in equity in 'Tata International (Thailand) Limited,' which recently became operational.

The principal role and responsibility of these TEL international subsidiaries was to promote the Tata brand in the region, develop international trade opportunities and strategic alliances and to assist in globalization of the Group companies' core businesses.

It gives me a great sense of satisfaction that the historical ties India shares with Africa were further cemented with the Tata Group playing the role of partners in progress. During this period, our main thrust was to build up relationships with various government and private sector organizations in Africa and expose them to Indian manufacturing capabilities in terms of plant and equipment.

The Tata foray into various geographies in Africa, gradually led me to several appointments which would further bring about closer ties between the two countries, promote business, build good relationship with the national governments and help improve the needs of the local African community.

I was appointed a member of the President's Investors' Advisory Council of Tanzania, Ghana and Uganda. I was also appointed Honorary Consul of Namibia, and had the honour to co-chair the 16th World Economic Forum on Africa in 2006.

Dr Essop Pahad, minister in the Presidency, Republic of South Africa, referred to me as a committed African, a kind, compassionate and caring individual, whose work as an individual and on behalf of the Tata Group in many countries on the continent of Africa was exemplary.

We developed a good standing and a name for ourselves in

Africa. During my tenure at TEL, Tata Africa grew from a business of US$3 million in 2004 to US$35 million in 2008 (PBT). With a view to increase our international presence and businesses, we entered into collaborations with reputed industrial groups worldwide in various business sectors, as seen in the next chapter.

Chapter 7

STRATEGIC ALLIANCES AND ASSOCIATIONS

I had returned from Singapore with a strong sense of nationalism and an idealistic desire to do something worthwhile for India. I knew there was plenty of scope in a country with a large population. I noticed that in spite of established high-quality educational institutes, we hardly had any industries that could be considered hi-tech. We had already lost the semi-conductor industry to newer economies in South-East Asia.

We, at Tata, felt one way to place India on the world's technology map and boost its reputation would be to collaborate with large corporations, research labs and institutes. I had remained in touch with Imperial College right from the day I left the institution. My correspondence with Prof. Ford not only inspired me, but my occasional meetings with him kept me abreast of new happenings and innovations in the engineering world. He would make it a point to send me information on new developments about materials and other related fields including medical electronics.

I also had access to British Petroleum (BP) and Rolls Royce.

Prof. Ford was a consultant to BP then and many students from Imperial College had taken up jobs with both these organizations. We did not do any business initially with Rolls Royce, but just kept in touch. Eventually, we persuaded them to come to India and look at some options for collaboration.

Of course, today, international companies come to India instead of us approaching them. However, in those pre-liberalization days, when the Indian government was still considering opening up the economy, big international names in the corporate world did not know much about Indian industries. They were not aware about Tatas' businesses to even consider us in the range of hi-tech industries.

We therefore started putting together our plans for collaboration and cooperation with international entities. We approached large companies like American Insurance Group (AIG), Rolls Royce, BP, United Technology and many others, to do business with India. Fortunately, we knew some of them because of our business associations from Singapore. Yet, it was an uphill challenge. For instance, it took four years to get a licence in 1989 for the Tata-BP Solar joint venture. The licensing for AIG also took years to materialize and due to all these delays, we had to design a different arrangement to work with AIG. Our opting for AIG was not only for the insurance business but also to explore other possible opportunities in IT, engineering and call centres. In spite of delays, I had a taste of fast-moving technology and we also experienced the excitement and fun of creating new breakthroughs for our country.

In a closed-door economy, we had commercial links with the UK and Germany, but the US was relatively unknown to India, the Tatas or any other Indian corporation. So, we tried to forge that link and develop a relationship.

Ratan had introduced me to Don De Marino, the gentleman

who retired as a senior official in the George H.W. Bush administration and we endured a good relationship. So, when we started a representative office in the US in the early 1990s, it was Don's job to scout around for business, technology and cooperation. He understood our thinking and we shared the common conviction that two of the largest democracies must also share a good political and business relationship.

Much later, in November 2007, I was invited to give a talk at Maryland University on how the relationship between the two nations grew to mutual benefit. Looking back historically, I can see that the Tatas' connect with the US started shaping in 1897–98 when Jamsetji first visited the US to procure talent for the steel plant. During the same time, Swami Vivekananda gave his first speech in Chicago.

There is an interesting story about these two great Indians. In 1897, on a boat that sailed from Yokohama to Vancouver, a monk and an industrialist met for the first time. The monk was Swami Vivekananda, who was to take and interpret to the West, more effectively than anyone else, the religious and philosophical traditions of India. The industrialist was Jamsetji Tata, who earned the sobriquet of the father of Indian industry. As they got talking, Vivekananda explained his mission of taking to the US the message of the universality of all religions. Jamsetji said he was in search of equipment and technology that would build the steel industry and make India a strong industrial nation. Vivekananda blessed Jamsetji, and remarked, 'How wonderful it would be if we could combine the scientific and technological achievements of the West with the asceticism and humanism of India!' They never met again after that journey. But these words struck a chord in Jamsetji's heart. Subsequently, Jamsetji wrote a letter to Vivekananda. I reproduce an excerpt from that letter below:

Esplanade House, Bombay.
23 November 1898

Dear Swami Vivekananda,

I trust, you remember me as a fellow traveller on your voyage from Japan to Chicago. I very much recall at this moment your views on the growth of the ascetic spirit in India, and the duty, not of destroying, but of diverting it into useful channels.

I recall these ideas in connection with my scheme of Research Institute of Science for India, of which you have doubtless heard or read. It seems to me that no better use can be made of the ascetic spirit than the establishment of monasteries or residential halls for men dominated by this spirit, where they should live with ordinary decency and devote their lives to the cultivation of sciences—natural and humanistic. I am of the opinion that, if such a crusade in favour of an asceticism of this kind were undertaken by a competent leader, it would greatly help asceticism, science, and the good name of our common country; and I know not who would make a more fitting general of such a campaign than Vivekananda. Do you think you would care to apply yourself to the mission of galvanizing into life our ancient traditions in this respect?

Vivekananda was busy starting the Ramakrishna Mission and could not accept the offer but he promptly sent his disciple Sister Nivedita who met Jamsetji and his advisor, Padsha. A detailed plan formulated by them was promptly suppressed by the Viceroy, Lord Curzon. However, the Tatas persevered and continued to work on their plans.

Vivekananda died in July 1902 and Jamsetji in 1904. Jamsetji's vision was realized five years later. Indian Institute of Science, Bangalore, a gift from the Tatas, was established in 1909 and is the pride of the nation today.

There were many nationalists who had to leave India, and many of them moved to the US. One of them was Noni Gopal Bose. His son, the world-famous scientist and engineer, Prof. Amar Gopal Bose, founder and chairman of Bose Corporation, was a great friend and admirer of Ratan.

I believe that while diplomats did a lot of work to build Indo-US relationship, it was Indian students who went there in the 1960s, who became the torch bearers. Earlier, most Indians would go to the UK for studies, but when fees were significantly raised by the then Prime Minister Margaret Thatcher, Indians started to look towards the US that welcomed them and offered scholarships.

Then came the charge of the software and IT industry in the 1980s, that further strengthened this relationship and brought tremendous recognition to India as a nation of talented software engineers with their knowledge of mathematics and computer science. Today many Indians teach in US universities and Indian doctors and scientists are to be found all over the country. The head honchos of top US businesses today are Indians too. Yet, in those days, Marino and I initiated a reverse process to persuade US companies to come to India.

We at TEL, focused on promoting export-oriented businesses in sunrise sectors through strategic alliances for global technology. The company chose futuristic high-tech businesses with a growing global market and high-entry barriers in terms of technology and capital. Some stories of our alliances are interesting. Like how the Tatas brought solar energy into the private sector in India for the first time around 1989–91.

Going Green with BP

I was always interested in clean energy for India and considered solar electricity as an alternative to huge conventional electrical plants. Years earlier, in the mid-1970s while in the US, I had visited NASA along with my brother and observed the Sputnik, which had just returned from space. This device was run on solar electricity and the body was built of composites. That sparked my imagination, but I had to wait several years for an opportunity to return to India and take my idea forward.

In the meantime, I gathered information about the ongoing R&D work in solar energy worldwide as well as the possibilities, besides learning about major players in this nascent industry. It was a futuristic industry and I found that BP was a significant player, doing a lot of R&D work. I touched upon the subject with Prof. Ford, who was also a consultant at BP, and he arranged a meeting for me with Bob Malfers, then managing director of BP, to explore the possibility of a joint venture with the Tatas.

Subsequently, I discussed the project with Ratan and Palkhivala and they encouraged me. When I spoke about solar energy with Moolgaokar, with a twinkle in his eyes he said, 'Syamal, you go ahead.' He also mentioned that being a new project, not much was known about it in the Group. It was hence important that our vision was clear—it had to be a new, sunrise industry, futuristic with a high entry barrier in terms of technology, money and management besides having a global market.

Being a technology man, Moolgaokar asked me, 'What else did you see in NASA? What else are they doing at Imperial?' He had a probing mind and always wanted to know more about advances happening around the world. That eager curiosity encouraged me to learn more and to keep myself abreast of developments in the technological world. Medical electronics was another subject that interested both him and Ratan. We finally decided to venture into the area of alternative energy with BP. Being a new job, we needed a good person to take charge of the project. We identified Arun Vora, then working with NELCO to lead this project. Although, he had no knowledge or background about solar photovoltaics, he got down to studying and understanding the field.

When we started our joint venture with BP in 1989, no other Indian private-sector player was engaged in solar energy. CEL and BHEL were doing some minor jobs, but with BP's global market access and technology, we had a good chance of success. Tata BP Solar was a small entity in the giant house of Tatas, but it was a step in the right direction. Vora was given the leadership and he handpicked the rest of his team.

We applied for the licence and it was Vora and Andrew Peers, a representative of BP, who really did the job for the joint venture company and made it a remarkable success. They got the licence and we started operations from a business centre in Bangalore. Once we received the approval from the government of India, we set up a state-of-the-art manufacturing facility of solar cells in a new building in Bangalore, commencing production in 1991. This is the place we started producing solar cells from silicon wafers.

Innovation drove the organization. For instance, in the initial years, as an experiment for application of knowledge, we put up a 100-KW unit at Valvan Dam of Tata Power in Lonavla, Maharashtra. It was the biggest plant in those days and is still running successfully. I am sure the capital investment has paid off long ago.

We also indigenously developed some new and affordable solar solutions such as the WHO-approved solar powered vaccine refrigerator, solar water pumping systems for irrigation, solar water heaters and solar lanterns, which Tata BP Solar introduced in India as one of the pioneers of the products. Some of these products like the refrigerators and lanterns could be effectively used in

Indian villages. We sold many lanterns all over the country, and in Ladakh, we lit 11,000 homes! However, marketing our products in India was not an easy task as these products that worked with solar energy were new and unfamiliar. Once in a while, few items like small photovoltaic power plants were ordered by public-sector organizations under government tenders.

There was a lot of excitement for me personally in this venture. My idea was not just to bring solar photovoltaic to India, but also be open to new technologies that the process would necessitate. As we were an export company and our major activities centred on exporting manufactured products out of India, we could not afford to lose track of this business. Exporting Tata BP products to cater to the demand, however small, to Europe and Japan was logical. Hence, I told the BP team that the best way to succeed commercially would be to sell our products overseas. The team was responsive and unafraid to develop new and creative products in-house. Soon, we exported 75 per cent of the production from Tata BP Solar globally, much more than what we sold in the Indian market. I am proud of Tata BP Solar, which we built up from scratch.

Despite the uncertainty and scepticism about our new and unfamiliar products, Tata BP's instant commercial success could be attributed to a good partnership with BP, aided by the oil price hike, and the fact that solar energy is pollution-free, clean, renewable and sustainable. Another big advantage was that it could easily 'travel' to the remotest of villages. I am grateful that though I was with TEL, a trading company, Moolgaokar always encouraged and supported me for technically innovative projects.

A Showcase for New Business

As Tata BP grew, several delegations from Africa, Europe and the US visited the plant. Gordon Brown, the then prime minister of

Britain, also visited the BP Solar Plant at Bangalore. Another time, Sir John Rose, the chief executive and managing director of Rolls Royce visited Tata BP Solar for an insight into the workings of a joint venture and what it entailed. He mentioned that he would bring 150 of his top managers as he was trying to convince them to do business in Asia and South-East Asia to gainfully use the price advantage and growing markets in this part of the globe.

Sir John and his team visited the plant and in that meeting he told me, 'Syamal, help me to change the attitude of my people. They need to accept that there are markets abroad, there are technologies abroad and there are tremendous possibilities for cooperation.'

It was a time when Rolls Royce had a lot of business in Europe and the US and the top management was thinking of coming to Asia. That evening, Sir John hosted a dinner for his staff members. Like Ratan and me, there were other guests too, like the chairman of HAL. One of the guests asked Ratan how the Tata BP Solar joint venture functioned, and how we managed the whole operation. Ratan referred the guest to me to answer. I did mention how difficult it was to run a JV, but at the same time how mutually beneficial a venture like this had turned out, by bringing out the best that both sides could offer. Like maintaining the stringent standards of BP International for solar cells, while manufacturing the panels locally in India.

Although there was no legal tie-up with Rolls Royce, its ancillary unit in Austria enjoyed some good business with Tata Advance Materials, one of the Tata companies. Sir John often visited us over the years and on many occasions, I invited Ratan to join us. Several years later, after my retirement, I got a call from the chairman's office to join him for dinner at The Chambers in the Taj Mahal Hotel, Mumbai, to meet Sir John. I was surprised as I was not aware Sir John was in town. Ratan and I had been meeting

Sir John together for the past 25–30 years. On this occasion, it was a last-minute call to check if I could join them. Since I was at the Taj that evening for other work, I went along to The Chambers for dinner.

When I arrived, I heard Sir John was passing through Mumbai. He seemed pleased on being invited for dinner and at the prospect of meeting both of us. All three of us had a lively discussion, just like it used to be in the old days. We talked about many things including what Sir John would do when he retire. It was just a relaxed evening.

I drove back with Ratan in his car and I said to him, 'Boss, it was kind of you to invite me to meet with Sir John.' He replied, 'Syamal, you and I have been with Sir John all these years. You are a friend of mine so it is only natural that you should be there.' I was surprised; I was no longer in business with Sir John, but Ratan had remembered to include me for the meeting. I was deeply touched by his gesture.

BP Solar too was so happy with the Bangalore unit that it requested us to depute Vora to help them in their global solar business. Vora did a splendid job as a member of BP's UK team for their solar photovoltaic business.

Vora captured my days with Tata BP Solar succinctly, though generously too. His words are a reflection of how I was groomed by my seniors and the support that my colleagues on the Board profusely extended to me. Let me repeat here in his words how he felt about the time we worked together:

> I have known and worked with Syamal Gupta for a long time—
> since 1984! There are many unforgettable memories in my
> association with Gupta. The most abiding collage of memories
> still remains that of a personality that is intensely humane;
> who deeply and genuinely cares for the people he comes in
> contact with; one who is highly interested in technology and

innovation—not only being brought to India from outside, but also in our Indian colleagues developing and excelling in them; one who can take a long term view of business, technology, people development and the interdependence amongst the three; above all someone who can rise above the present, above the near term obstacles, above the many 'thorns and inevitable pitfalls in the path of a pioneer.' These aspects of his personality have been a great source of inspiration to all those who genuinely want to do something significant in life.

'Technology and Innovation are subjects that are close to Gupta's heart. His keen desire to make solar energy accessible to the rural population living in remote, isolated villages was translated by Tata BP Solar into products specially developed to cater to the 'bottom of the pyramid.' Again, encouraged by Gupta, Tata BP Solar has developed comprehensive Solar Solution Packages for rural health, rural education, rural telecom and integrated rural development that have major implications, not just for India, but for all those developing countries, where lack of access to clean, affordable and reliable energy continues to be a challenge for a vast majority.

Gupta's outstanding contribution is also clearly evident in the milestone projects executed by Tata BP Solar in the South Asian region. These projects, executed under his leadership, are especially noteworthy for the sea-change they have brought into the lives of the end-users and for serving as catalysts for the socio-economic development of the region, empowering women, enhancing opportunities for income generating activities, bridging the urban-rural digital divide in education that are all in synergy with the Tata group's philosophy of 'improving the quality of life.'

The former managing director of BP, Bryan K. Sanderson, wrote to me on my retirement as chairman of Tata BP Solar:

You can retire with great pride in your achievement in taking solar power from little more than a laboratory experiment to its current place at the heart of the alternative energy programme.

Our joint venture with BP led us into new areas of cooperation. In the year 2000, at a meeting in Chicago to review our solar business with BP, I had the opportunity to meet Dr Phiroze Darukhanavala, the newly appointed vice president and chief technology officer of BP America, who incidentally was a Tata Scholar, an awardee of the J.N. Tata Endowment scholarship. Darukhanavala expressed satisfaction about our solar business in Bangalore and assured all support from BP.

When Darukhanavala informed me about BP's Digital and Engineering Business Group (EBG) with an annual budget of $2 billion, it immediately sparked a thought and I offered to introduce TCS for BP's India operations. Darukhanavala was surprised that the Tatas were into the IT sector and showed interest in this tie up. I immediately arranged for presentations by TCS and Tata Infotech in the US.

Thereafter, Kohli and S. Ramadorai from TCS successfully interacted with BP and were able to secure some good business. I knew Ramadorai as a young technocrat in TCS. Over the years, he became CEO of TCS in 1996 and contributed significantly towards the development and growth of the company to its present position. He always helped people in need—on or off the job.

Several rounds of interactions between the two businesses resulted in a concrete business proposal in 2002, when BP outsourced from TCS services in the areas of IT and software, call centres, accounting and financial services. User managers within BP were impressed with the services provided by TCS. BP outsourcing from India at that time was valued at $1 billion. However, apart from TCS, BP started to outsource IT services from other Indian companies in later years. Our relationship with BP was cordial and expanded into new areas from time to time.

As per the terms of agreement, BP and Tata were to nominate chairmanship of the JV in alternate years. However when BP's turn came, they requested me to continue as chairman of the company. I continued in this positions for the next 25 years. In this period, we managed to institute a scholarship for Indian students to further their studies in M.Sc. in the UK, to be funded jointly by the JV partners.

We also promoted distant learning programmes for M.Tech through Virginia Polytechnic Institute and State University, USA, in association with the S.P. Jain Institute of Management and Research, Mumbai.

Partnership with AIG

Exploring strategic alliances across the borders, we were eyeing a few international companies for collaboration in the insurance sector and one of them was AIG. Once again, TEL played a pivotal role in this significant Tata initiative. AIG was into leasing finance for aircrafts, trading in gold and commodities, and involved in finance business.

Several meetings were held between the Tatas and the top management of AIG in which De Marino played a pivotal role. Finally, in April 1993, following the preliminary discussions, we arranged a high-level meeting between Ratan and AIG chairman, Maurice 'Hank' Greenberg. It was decided at this meeting that Tata and AIG will explore possibilities of cooperation while we wait for the insurance sector to open up in India. In the interim, we explored possibilities of a joint venture. Apparently, Greenberg was impressed with Ratan and his future plans for the Tatas and cooperation with AIG. Further, Greenberg requested Ratan to join his international Board of Advisors, which was a great recognition.

They often met in the US, and on other international boards to take forward their common goal of globalization.

An MOU was signed in January 1995 between Tatas and AIG in the presence of Brown, then Secretary of Commerce, USA, who was in Delhi. Subsequently, a cooperation agreement was signed by Ratan and Greenberg. Thereafter, negotiations started. From the Tatas, there was me, F.K. Kavarana, Ishaat Hussain and Soonawala and from AIG, Charles Boulox and a few others. We had long meetings in Mumbai, London and New York with lawyers from both sides locked in intense discussions.

AIG wanted to be the majority shareholder and we could not agree to that. We offered a 50:50 arrangement, but felt the Indian government may not allow us to go ahead with it. I ended up playing a crucial role in these negotiations. I would go and meet Greenberg once in a while. Without any in-depth knowledge of law or the business of insurance, it was slow, yet persistent persuasion tactics that we followed.

One day, it struck me that AIG was such a big insurance company, and wondered what they did about their IT. I suggested to them that they could set up their call centre in India. Greenberg showed interest. I told them they should talk to Kohli, the man behind TCS and India's IT revolution. Soon, Kohli and I met Greenberg. He was impressed. Kohli had meetings with the operating people for discussions to take the matter further. Eventually, TCS did get the IT business of AIG insurance, but it was a tough ride all along.

Ronald J. Anderson of AIG revisited India in the late 1980s. Having earlier worked in the General Insurance business in Mumbai, he wanted to assess the progress in the proposed joint venture. He had a chance meeting with Ratan when he discussed the Tata-AIG cooperation. Ratan told Anderson to meet me.

That night, Anderson met me for dinner at the Taj. Later,

he stated, 'The chemistry could not have been better. That was the beginning of a long journey where many things might have gone wrong, but Syamal Gupta, more than anyone else, held the relationship in place during the lead up to de-nationalization and the final partnership negotiations.'

Another enriching friendship was born when AIG and Tata were courting each other. Charles Boulox of AIG reminisced, 'The first time I met Syamal was in 1995 at the AIG offices in New York. I distinctly remember that from our first meeting itself, we were very friendly and I could tell that Syamal was a man who spoke from the heart...'

This courtship resulted in a happy marriage and finally the joint venture agreement between Tata and AIG was signed on 14 December 2000 and the company started business operation on 22 January 2001. In its very first year, Tata AIG's Life and General Insurance operations touched the lives of over half a million Indians. Frank Wisner, US Ambassador to India and Sunil Mehta for AIG, and N.A. Soonawala and Ishaat Hussain from Tata, played a big role in this joint venture.

Boulox remarked, 'Once Tata and AIG became partners, Syamal and I would meet regularly and our relationship has developed into a friendship that is a deeper bond than our business relationship. This elevation of business relationships into deep and abiding friendships that have stood the test of time, is another recurring motif in the life of Syamal Gupta. To him business is not important as relationships. People are more important.'

Later, my friend Don De Marino recounted, 'Together we helped bring some major US companies to India, something that seems effortless today, but which was quite a task back then. Syamal held a deep belief in the future potential of close ties between India and the US. At the advent of what is now finally becoming that deep relationship between the two great democracies, we all owe a great debt to men such as Syamal who saw it early and stayed the course.'

Today, I am happy to say that this business has grown significantly and has touched the lives of people in the country.

Tie-ups for Success

While we were engaged in many activities, there was persistent pressure from the government and also from within the Group to improve exports, especially for value-added products. I too was trying to improve the organizational culture, so that manufacturing became the base for exports. In my view, our own manufactured products were the future. Many opportunities for strategic collaborations came our way.

Holset: A British engineering company for Turbo chargers, Holset was a subsidiary of Cummins and they wanted to set up a plant in Pune. I had a meeting with Talaulicar, the managing director of Tata Motors. He was also on the TEL Board. I also had a series of meetings with Holset, London, and was ultimately able to convince them that Indore was an ideal location to set up this business. It was to be a joint venture between Holset, Tata Motors and TEL. Of course, the caveat was that exports, someday, would be conducted through TEL.

Asahi Glass: Next came an opportunity to work with a Japanese company, Asahi Glass, to make float glass. The Tatas was in steel and cement and I thought what was missing was glass. So, when the Asahi opportunity came our way, I took the initiative to start a joint venture with ACC and Tata Motors. ACC would use glass as construction material along with steel, and Tata Motors would use it for their vehicle windscreens.

I met the Asahi Glass team in Japan several times and convinced them to come to India. It was a win-win situation. The project came up in Mumbai and we had the export rights of their products. We exported to Africa and several other countries. We exited from this venture due to an internal management decision later, which I still regretted. We continue to export float glass to China and some African countries. Here was an opportunity, which could have grown big. My ultimate purpose of going into glass was that someday, the semi-conductor industry would use glass as material. Ratan whole-heartedly supported us in both these projects with Holset and Asahi Glass.

McDonnell Douglas: Earlier, when De Marino and I were meeting some big US companies to encourage them to set up business in India, we had visited AIG in relation to a helicopter deal with McDonnell Douglas Corporation, a major aerospace company. The helicopters were to be sold to African countries and in exchange, AIG wanted the Tatas to buy coffee and pay off the money. It was kind of a counter-trade deal and they wanted the Tatas to handle the process.

I went to McDonnell Douglas Corporation to study and examine the project details and to see what sort of business they operated. I was impressed with their helicopter with no tail rotor and invited Ratan, knowing his interest, to come and see the new technology. He liked the helicopter and decided to become a helicopter pilot.

A memorandum of agreement was signed between Tata Advanced Materials Limited (TAML) and McDonnell Douglas Corporation on 5 December 1996 for manufacture of helicopter components. This was the first time we met Harry C. Stonecipher, president and chief executive officer of the Corporation. There were possibilities of co-production of helicopters in India with TAML, which went on to become one of the first companies in India to be certified as an accredited manufacturer of composite materials, catering to the global aerospace, defence and industrial markets.

Several Tata Group companies exported to emerging markets in Africa, South America, West Asia, South-East Asia and also to developed countries in Europe and the US through the TEL network of overseas subsidiaries, liaison offices, branch offices and joint ventures abroad.

TEL focused on collaborations and promotion of export-oriented hi-tech businesses and even took a minority equity stake in some of them. The rationale was to enter sunrise industries ahead of competitors in order to influence and shape the industry evolution and international business landscape. The minority equity stake was taken selectively in order to have sustained international trading rights for the product or services of these new businesses in different countries.

When I came to TEL, my job was also to introduce myself and meet members from the CII, the Federation of Indian Export Organisations (FIEO), the Engineering Export Promotion Council, the Textile and Garment Council and other government organizations. I met officials of these trade bodies regularly to understand what policies they were going to implement.

Ratan introduced me to Tarun Das, director general of CII, whom he regarded as an interesting individual working hard towards its development to make it an international organization. Since then, Tarun became a good friend and supporter. He had deep knowledge of international trade and business and always advised me about the countries and businesses to which India's interests could be promoted. I have never seen him talk ill about anybody. He was always willing to help. He was instrumental in appointing me on some of the CII and governmental committees that helped the facilitation of export promotion of Indian goods and services through TEL.

I was on the CII committees for business development for the UK, US, South-East Asia, especially Singapore and many others.

I travelled to many countries like China, the US, the UK and Singapore with the ministerial delegations. As a member of CII, I got a chance to meet many industrialists. Though many of these interactions started as part of business networking, they often developed into friendships.

Some of the meetings had far-reaching repercussions. Once, when we went to China with former Prime Minister Dr Manmohan Singh, many important issues were discussed and a clear message was that we should develop stronger business ties with the country. I went to the US with Yashwant Sinha, the former finance minister and had meetings with various government officials, agencies, organizations and also with the Asiatic Society. Those were interesting and encouraging days—getting to know about the people, the development and forging of new policies influencing the future path of different industries. Most policy decisions influencing India's development were ultimately driven by relationships between the government and private industry and Tarun played an outstanding role in developing these vital business ties.

I once attended a lunch Tarun had organized in Delhi. I was impressed to see the galaxy in attendance. When I say galaxy, I mean in terms of value and quality and not in terms of position or wealth. They included industrialists like Ratan Tata, Arun Maira, Rahul Bajaj and Subodh Bhargava besides former Cabinet Secretary Naresh Chandra and many others. The gathering recognized Tarun's contribution to trade, industry and government. He simply won the hearts of people in India and abroad and despite all his achievements, remains his usual humble self. Tarun served the CII from 1967 to 2004. In 2006, the Government of India awarded him the Padma Bhushan, the third highest civilian honour for his contributions to Indian trade and industry.

Promoting Indo–Africa Relations

While I was actively involved with a number of CII committees, groups and sub-groups, it was decided that in line with the government's policy, we should have a separate committee for Africa. By that time the Tatas were fairly entrenched in Africa, though for CII it was just the beginning. Tatas had entered Africa 10 years earlier and by that time we had a presence in 10 to 15 African countries. As I had initiated and developed ties with a lot of people in the government and industry, I was selected to be the Founder Chairman of the Africa Committee of CII. We started work in earnest.

Tarun was the guiding spirit in the promotion of India–Africa business relations. He too pushed the agenda forward and managed to garner substantial support from the Government of India. Today, the Africa Committee on which I served for seven years, has grown in strength. After me, Sanjay Kirloskar served for two years, followed by Noel Tata. The Africa Committee is one of the most active in CII and is well recognized in Africa. Major Indian businesses that came to Africa were Godrej, Mahindra, Kirloskar Pumps and Shapoorji Pallonji Group.

The annual meetings of the India–Africa Conclave held by CII attracted large participation from both sides and several business deals were concluded culminating in a stronger business environment and cordial relations. I was also on the Board of Governors in the School of Oriental and African Studies, University of London. That is where a lot of discussions took place on Africa and where I would meet a number of African dignitaries.

Similarly, I met various people through the Commonwealth Business Council (CBC). Ratan had nominated me on the board and I continued to be part of it for a long time. At one meeting of the CBC Board held in Johannesburg, I had the opportunity to speak on sustainable development, sharing the dais with Goh Chok Tong, the former prime minister of Singapore. It was an interesting experience. I also co-chaired a meeting with the World Economic Forum in Johannesburg.

Another African initiative I was instrumental in forming was the Zambia International Business Advisory Council (ZIBAC). In February 2002, Mwanawasa, then the new president of Zambia approached the Tatas expressing the difficulty he was facing in attracting foreign investments in Zambia. He also found it hard to garner local support. He was seeking Tatas' involvement to further increase their investment in the country and assist them in attracting other investors. I thought over the matter and suggested forming an International Advisory Council consisting mainly of people from overseas, who would further enhance Zambia's cause through contacts with their associates, institutions and organizations.

I invited President Mwanawasa and his team to London and arranged meetings with prominent bankers, industrialists and businessmen, to form an international council. I also invited CBC office bearers, Lord Simon Cairns, the chairman and Mohan Kaul, director-general and CEO of the council, to join the group. It was formed to advise Zambia on how resources of the private sector like technology, finance and entrepreneurial skills could help them form a strategic vision. We would focus on specific areas—mining, power, tourism, agriculture, financial services and technology.

President Mwanawasa was pleased with the outcome and ZIBAC was formed, for which an inaugural meeting was held in Livingstone in September 2003. President Mwanawasa requested me to initially guide ZIBAC as Member. I continued to attend a few more meetings until I realized that my task was accomplished. ZIBAC continues to spearhead reform programmes in all sectors of the Zambian economy and aims to constantly improve the business and investment climate of the country.

Through my business association with the CBC and Commonwealth Development Council, the finance institution owned by the UK government, we were funding various projects in Africa and also meeting African dignitaries. TEL has built relationships with governments of several countries; financial institutions like Asian Development Bank, African Development Bank; and international agencies like EDB, Singapore.

In line with Tata Group's code of conduct and its statement of purpose, 'to improve the quality of life of citizens in the countries in which the Tata Group operates', TEL in India and its subsidiaries abroad have helped in the development plans of the host country and facilitated improvement in the quality of life of the citizens through employment generation and community-related initiatives in various countries.

Through its international operations, TEL also developed a large pool of competent and versatile managers with a global mindset from among its own officers and from other Tata Group companies besides several reputed supporting manufacturers, joint ventures and strategic alliance partners in various countries. While some of these managers are with the Tata Group today, several others are in prominent leadership positions in reputed companies worldwide including India.

As per the Tata Group guidelines, I laid down the mantle of managing director of TEL in 1999 upon reaching the age of 65 years. Thereafter, I was entrusted with the responsibility as chairman of the Board of TEL, a role from which I retired in 2009. Since then, the direction of TEL has changed many times under the new leadership. Each new incumbent has visualized the future of the company differently based on the expertise and experience he brought.

To sum up, my years with Tata Exports gave me tremendous opportunities to learn, to share, to grow and to impact business in my own small way with people in different corners of the world. Like TPI, TEL too gave me an opportunity to form the best of friendships worldwide, which I shall always cherish and treasure.

Chapter 8

LEAGUE OF LEADERSHIP

A large part of the Tata success story is the extraordinary people and professionals from diverse backgrounds that it supported. These individuals, with their work ethics, professional excellence and humility, subtly influenced the shaping of my career, my perspective and my personal life. With the passage of time, some of these professional associations gradually turned into deep personal relationships and life-long friendships.

I would hence like to record here my association with my senior colleagues at Tata, who were always a source of inspiration and guidance for me in my various responsibilities in the Group's companies, with whom I shared life-long friendships in addition to those who inspired me and deeply influenced my career at TISCO.

Paul Mueller

Paul Mueller, the chief engineer at TISCO, was an exceptional person whom I admired greatly. He could work on the drawing board as well as in the Works at ease. He was an engineering graduate from Germany, and worked with Schloemann, Germany, a rolling mill builder. Mueller was deputed to TISCO, Jamshedpur, sometime in the early 1930s to install a new Blooming Mill replacing the existing one. TISCO wanted the job to be done with minimal shut down of production. Mueller meticulously planned and worked on innovative techniques to complete this mammoth task in 52 hours. TISCO awarded a hefty bonus of ₹20,000 to Schloemann for this job.

Then came the Second World War that left Germany's economy in shambles. Soon thereafter, Paul Mueller returned to TISCO, Jamshedpur, and was subsequently appointed the chief engineer at CEDD. Though a young engineer, I was fortunate to watch Mueller work on many initiatives, particularly on the two-million-tonne expansion programme undertaken by TISCO and Kaizer Engineers.

I recall a chance meeting with Mueller one winter morning, at our office entrance. He told me that he had just visited Rourkela, Bhilai and Durgapur plants and that he was impressed. He further asked me, 'Gupta, have you been to Rourkela, Bhilai and Durgapur? New steel plants are coming up there and it would be a good idea to visit them and you will get some experience of the latest technology from the Germans, Russians and British without visiting Europe.'

I visited Bhilai and Rourkela. I was exposed to German and Russian plants, equipment and technology. It was a great experience for me to see, for the first time, the LD process of steel-making while we were still using the Bessemer process. Later, Tata Steel too adopted the LD process, which was a superior technology.

Harold Hodgekinson

An Englishman with sound structural and mechanical engineering knowledge, Harold Hodgekinson was highly experienced in stress analysis and engineering calculations. He was polite, humble and helpful by nature and was succeeded by K.P. Mahalingam when he retired.

K.P. Mahalingam

A topper in mechanical engineering from the erstwhile Victoria Jubilee Technical Institute (VJTI), Mumbai, K.P. Mahalingam joined TISCO as a graduate trainee in the Works and went on to become superintendent in the Machine Shop. He was a bright engineer and secured the coveted Indo–German scholarship for advanced training in Germany. He was trained at Maschinenfabrik Sack which I too had joined in later years.

Paul Mueller had earlier met Mahalingam in Germany and was impressed with his professional ability and talent. Mueller invited Mahalingam to join CEDD after which he was transferred from Works to CEDD. With his background in Works and also Sack in Germany, Mahalingam proved to be an asset to the steel company and was later appointed the chief engineer.

Incidentally, when I was in London in the early 1960s, studying at the Imperial College, it was Mahalingam who went out of his way to recommend my case to S.K. Nanavati, the managing director, to sponsor my postgraduate studies.

Over time, our professional relationship evolved into a personal one. The Mahalingams were the first to invite us home for get-togethers in Jamshedpur. My wife Chandra also recalls their stay with us while I was with TPI, Singapore. We had a great time together.

Ratan Tata became a close friend of Mahalingam and whenever we were in Mumbai together, Ratan would have us over for a meal. On Mahalingam's ninetieth birthday, Ratan made it a point to fly to Chennai to personally greet him.

Dr Homi N. Sethna

Homi N. Sethna, a nuclear scientist and ex-chairman of the Atomic Energy Commission, was appointed chairman of the Tata Power

Companies and invited by J.R.D. Tata to join the Board of Tata Sons Ltd.

Initially, Sethna invited me to join the Board of Tata Power companies and later, he took keen interest in my work in Tata International Ltd, when we interacted on several international businesses of the company. He further recommended me to head Tata Consulting Engineers and Tata Projects as chairman. He always promoted engineering and good engineers and had a good long-term vision for nuclear power. He guided Tata Power, Tata Projects and Tata Consulting Engineers to greater heights.

A sound engineer, Sethna was practical in his approach, and internationally known as a nuclear scientist who contributed significantly towards the development and growth of Indian atomic research.

Jamshed K. Setna

Jamshed K. Setna was a highly qualified chartered accountant and a Fellow of the Institute of Chartered Accountants of India, who served major international companies in India in the top positions. He was chairman of Colgate India and Ingersoll-Rand (India). Setna was invited to join the Board of Tata Sons Ltd. He brought to the Board his rich experience and understanding of the Indian industry and consumer business.

In my association with him on the Board of Tata Sons and Tata International, I found him to be an extremely thorough gentleman who always promoted good systems of governance. Setna guided me as chairman of Tata International towards its developmental growth. He always made time to meet business partners of TIL in India and abroad and played an important role in the growth of the Group. Our professional relations finally turned into a life-long close family friendship which I greatly cherish.

K.M. Chinnappa

K.M. Chinnappa was the managing director of the erstwhile Tata Electric Companies (TEC) and ably led and guided the power companies in difficult times. He was also at the helm of Tata Consulting Engineers, Tata Projects and Tata Advanced Materials Limited.

A committed individual with a friendly disposition, with whom I also worked closely at TCE and TAML, he was a sincere Tata man and a skilled engineer with superior people-management qualities.

H.P. Bodhanwala

A graduate from Pune University in civil and structural engineering, H.P. Bodhanwala started his career in the design office in CEDD, TISCO. He gradually moved up the ladder to be the chief design engineer at a young age and contributed significantly to the development and implementation of the two-million-tonne expansion programme. Subsequently, he was promoted as chief engineer and finally as executive director of the company.

A highly respected figure in Jamshedpur, he also promoted sports, welfare, yoga and education. A good human being, warm and generous by nature, he would go out of his way to help people and played an active role in the modernization of the Tata Main Hospital and the blood bank in Jamshedpur. He was also associated with the Jamshedpur Chapter of the Indian Institute of Engineers.

Pheroze Tarapore

Pheroze Tarapore, a mechanical engineer from Manchester, joined the Project Department of TISCO and moved his way up in the organization. We remember him as a person who always encouraged us to devote time at the library and upgrade ourselves with the latest technology and development. Tarapore was pushing us to do more in this fast-moving world of technology and we owe our professional growth and that of the company to him.

EPILOGUE

By the time this book is published, I would have crossed my 86th birthday. So I need to explain why I felt compelled to write this book. The reader can be sure that it is not for royalties or fame. What will I do with them at this age?

I have been a part of a unique phase of India's economic journey—the years where the private sector broke loose from domestic fetters to spread both overseas and into new high-tech sectors. I wanted to write that wonderful story from the point of view of an insider, as a Tata man.

It has been my privilege to be a part of the House of Tata for 55 years. The Tata Group has been a path-breaker in many fields; it has built the foundation that India and Indians now take for granted.

I have been, as my close friend R. Gopalakrishnan delights in calling me, one of those working on new paths and indeed, one of the bricklayers of the Tata Group. This book is about a bricklayer's perspective of how those were important years, from the 1970s onwards.

My role at Tata was a mixed bag of experiences—lots of technology development, quite a bit of developing international trade networks, a lot of effort in nurturing new joint ventures, and finally, securing a place for Tata in new geographies.

I wanted to share the story of how this group spread its wings and entered new territories. In the current business environment, surely there is an opportunity to tell a true, heart-warming account of those years. I hope this book is able to do so.

This, then, is my small contribution to Indian business history. I hope my effort will be rewarded by the curiosity of future managers. After all, neither Rome nor Tata was built in a day! Who would know that better than the bricklayers?

ACKNOWLEDGEMENTS

Compiling the textual material of this autobiography from my letters and notes preserved over the years and from developments recorded in Tata House journals, has been a journey in itself. Starting in 2013 with several sittings of audio recordings of my experiences in the Tata Group, delving into memories of professional and personal encounters and interactions, committing these transcriptions on to paper, followed by countless redrafted pages, have taken a long stretch of time. My colleagues, executive assistants and secretaries at Tata International have worked tirelessly to shape the text and compile the chapters.

Here, I would like to acknowledge each one of them individually for their unstinted support while bearing with my demand for time: Kamalrukh Baria, Shaman Agarwal, Amrita Banerjee, Elva Gonsalves, Meher Edibam, Kainaz Mistry and Sneha Panthaki. My daughter, Debjani Sen, further assisted me in the edit of the text to finalize the first rough draft—all of sheer woman-power at work!

Fershoger Guard, a retired colleague, assisted in re-editing and finalization task to put this book together for me!

To all my colleagues and friends in Singapore and Africa, for sharing material towards the compilation of this book.

To the Tata Central Archives, Pune, for their assistance in sharing the required photographs for publication.

To Rupa Publications, for releasing the autobiography in this beautiful presentation.

INDEX

ABC Bearings, 51
Agrico, 44
agricultural, 44, 45, 52, 107, 113, 122, 126, 128, 141
American Insurance Group (AIG), 153, 164, 165, 166, 168
Asahi Glass, 167, 168
Ash, Eric, 35, 36
Azbeck, Dr, 19, 22, 26

Bhatnagar, B.S., 106
Bickley, Prof., FRS, 27
Black Economic Empowerment programme, 145
Blackett, Patrick (Prof.), 28
Bodhanwala, H. P., 11, 12, 14, 179
Bose, Subhas Chandra, 39
British Petroleum (BP), 116, 117, 152
Brouillet, Robert, 120, 121

CBC, 171, 172, 173
CEDD, 6, 7, 8, 9, 13, 29, 40, 48, 53, 176, 177, 179
Chandra, 20, 26, 39, 90, 96, 170, 177
Chatterjee, P.K., 8, 12
Chinnappa, K.M., 179
coal, 38, 39, 116, 117, 149

Commonwealth Business Council (CBC), 171
Confederation of Indian Industry (CII), 95
continuous productivity improvement, 95

Dasgupta, S., 9
DBS, 59, 60, 84, 88
Demag, 12, 13, 14, 19
Deora, Murli, 89
design office, 7, 8, 10, 22, 180
Development Bank of Singapore (DBS), 59
Dhanabalan, 59, 60, 84
Dhawan, Raman, 127, 136, 138, 143, 144
Dr Goh, 54, 55, 56, 59, 60, 64

Economic Development Board (EDB), 56
EDB, 56, 57, 58, 59, 60, 61, 62, 64, 67, 68, 69, 70, 75, 81, 84, 92, 93, 95, 96, 98, 173
emerging technology, 109
expansion, 5, 8, 9, 10, 12, 16, 19, 22, 51, 62, 79, 114, 124, 128, 130, 145, 148, 176, 180
export, 50, 55, 61, 89, 101, 104, 105,

106, 107, 108, 112, 113, 114, 115, 118, 124, 127, 137, 138, 141, 144, 156, 159, 168, 169

FEMA, 107
Fishery, 114, 132
footwear division, 122
Ford, Hugh (Prof.), 27, 28, 33, 36, 85, 86, 157
foreign exchange, 41, 42, 60, 61, 63, 101, 104, 105, 109, 130, 140
Foreign Exchange Regulation Act (FERA), 107
foreign investment, 57, 61
Founder's statue, 17, 18
free market economy, 56, 96, 100

Gandhi, Indira, 16, 17
GE, 57, 58, 69, 70, 71, 72, 77
globalization, 53, 84, 99, 106, 124, 150, 165
Goh Keng Swee, 54, 55, 64
Greenberg, 164, 165
Grootenhuis, Prof., 28, 33
Growth Shop, 41, 42
Gupta-Ford formula, 33
Gupta, Syamal, ix, x, 14, 30, 33, 35, 36, 37, 44, 74, 80, 83, 84, 85, 86, 92, 93, 105, 142, 157, 160, 161, 166, 167

Hanover Industrial Fair, 24
Hayles, Bill, 25, 29, 30
higher education and training, 97
Holset, 167, 168

Imperial College, 16, 25, 26, 27, 29, 32, 33, 34, 35, 36, 37, 71, 152, 153, 177
import, 40, 41, 42, 43, 44, 48, 49, 50, 69, 106, 107, 115, 116, 117, 124, 137, 149
Indian National Academy of Engineers (INAE), 16

Industrial and Mining Development Bank of Iran, 53
Institution of Mechanical Engineers (IMechE), 16
International Investors' Round Table Conference, 148
international market, 50, 78, 79, 108, 109, 119
International Monetary Fund, 148
Intraco, 90, 96

Jadavpur University, 3, 4
joint venture, 44, 54, 60, 62, 81, 82, 87, 90, 132, 142, 145, 153, 157, 158, 160, 163, 164, 165, 166, 167
JPC, 48, 51, 112
JRD, 7, 17, 21, 44, 47, 51, 54, 55, 56, 60, 79, 82, 83, 84, 85, 86, 88, 94, 102
Jubilee Park, 17, 18
Jurong Industrial Town, 62
JV, 160, 164

Kaizer Engineers, 8, 176
Kajal, 25, 26, 92
Kaul, O.K., 119, 121, 122, 172
Kaunda, Kenneth, 129, 130, 132
Kavarana, Farrokh, 54, 79, 94, 120, 165
Kersting, Emile, 9, 21, 22, 23, 26
Kirloskar pumps, 113
Kohli, Faqir Chand, 89
Kutar, Firoze, 13, 43, 44

Larsen and Toubro, 74
Leather, 102, 117, 118, 119, 120, 121, 122, 123
Leather division, 118, 119, 120, 122, 123
Leather Finishing, 117, 119, 121
Lee Kuan Yew, 54, 55, 100
licence, 48, 82, 107, 118, 153, 158
Luangwa Bicycle Industries, 131

Mahalingam, K.P., 13, 15, 29, 40, 42,

44, 176, 177

Maira, Arun, 56, 58, 60, 80, 82, 102

Makumbi Agricultural and Tractor
Company (MATCO), 128

Malgham, 104, 105, 115, 134

Marino, Don De, 153, 166

Maschinenfabrik Sack GmBH, 9

MATCO, 128

Mbeki, Thabo, 144, 145

Mbeki, Zanele, 146

McDonnell Douglas, 168

Mehta, Freddie, 54, 60, 83

minerals, 127, 135, 147, 149

mining equipment, 139

Mistry, Pallonji, 108

Mitsubishi, 109, 110, 117

Moolgaokar, Sumant, ix, 24, 80, 86

Mueller, Paul, 6, 11, 12, 14, 15, 22, 175,
176, 177

Mukherjee, Pranab, 88

Muthuraman, B, 18, 95

Mwanawasa, Levy, 140, 172

Nanavati, S. K., 15, 16, 29, 30, 41, 42,
47, 51, 53, 177

NASA, 92, 93, 157

Nathan, S.R., 94, 95, 96

Nehru, Jawaharlal, 5, 16, 39, 125, 147

open-door policy, 94

overseas, 10, 36, 41, 49, 50, 52, 53, 60,
95, 109, 111, 112, 115, 129, 149,
159, 169, 172, 181

Palkhivala, N, 82, 86, 87, 88, 90, 102,
108, 109, 132, 157

Pamodzi, 127, 135, 139, 140, 145

Paris Leather Show, 120

partnering with governments, 131

Permanent Resident Scheme, 80

Philips, 57, 58, 69

Pock Too, Ng, 59, 64, 95, 96, 98

pollution control, 97, 119

PP computers (also PP machines), 92

pre-liberalized India, 136

Qazi, Abinava, 56, 58, 65, 85

Rao, D.V., 11

R&D, 32, 43, 44, 110, 119, 157

Reuter, Hans, 14

Ring Rolling Mill, 49

Rollei, 69, 72

Rolling Mill, 49

Rolls Royce, 31, 152, 153, 160

Rose, Sir John, 160

Royal Academy of Engineering, 16, 36

Sack, Dr, 9, 19, 21, 22, 23, 25, 26, 177

Santhals, 18

scholarship for Indian students, 164

School of Oriental and African Studies,
143, 171

Seagate, 75, 76

semi-conductor, 58, 66, 69, 71, 72, 74,
75, 78, 91, 152, 168

Sethna, Homi (Dr), 43, 116, 177

Setna, Jamshed K., 178, 179

Shaikh, F.M.A., 68

Shapoorji Pallonji Group, 171

Siemens, 57, 58, 69, 72, 73

Sime Darby, 58, 60, 63, 88

Smith Corona, 74, 76, 77

solar, 110, 114, 156, 157, 158, 159, 160,
161, 162, 163

Soonawala, Noshir A., 93, 94, 165,
166,

Star Wars programme, 93

strip mill, 22, 23

sub-Saharan Africa, 126, 145, 148

sunrise industries, 71, 169

Svenska Kullagerfabriken (SKF), 47, 48,
50, 51

Tandon Inc., 76

Tarapore, Pheroze, 17, 180

Tata Advanced Materials Limited
(TAML), 168, 179

Tata Africa Holdings, South Africa, 145, 149

Tata BP Solar, 153, 158, 159, 160, 161, 162

Tata Consultancy Services (TCS), 82

Tata Consulting Engineers (TCE), 90

Tata-Cope Allman, 81

Tata Dalgety, 54

Tata, Dorabji, 39

Tata Elxsi, 90, 92

Tata Exports, x, 24, 35, 36, 56, 101, 102, 104, 105, 106, 107, 109, 136, 173

Tata Farms and Foods, 141

Tata Government Training Centre (TGTC), 67

Tata Holdings (Tanzania), 148, 149, 150

Tata Incorporated, 53

Tata International AG, 60

Tata, Jamsetji (see also Jamsetji), xi, 17, 18, 38, 39, 154, 155

Tata Limited, 25, 29, 53, 126

Tata Man (also, Tata men), 30, 91

Tata Motors, 41, 82, 102, 111, 112, 116, 138, 141, 145, 148, 167

Tata, Noel, 115, 116, 122, 171

Tata Powers, 89, 98, 113, 116, 117, 158, 178

Tata Precision Industries (TPI), 24

Tata, Ratan, x, xii, 18, 19, 40, 41, 42, 44, 45, 46, 47, 53, 54, 75, 83, 91, 92, 93, 94, 95, 102, 108, 124, 126, 140, 142, 144, 145, 146, 153, 156, 157, 158, 160, 161, 164, 165, 168, 169, 170, 171, 177

Tata Sons, x, xii, 7, 18, 24, 60, 80, 92, 93, 94, 108, 178, 179

Tata trucks, 111, 138, 149

Tata Zambia, 124, 126, 127, 128, 138, 149

Tata Zambia Limited (TZL), 126

Tata Zug, 54, 79

tax subsidies, 106

TCE, 90, 179

TCS, 82, 89, 90, 98, 124, 145, 146, 163, 165

TEL, 90, 101, 102, 103, 104, 105, 106, 107, 108, 109, 110, 111, 112, 113, 114, 115, 117, 118, 119, 120, 121, 122, 123, 124, 126, 128, 129, 131, 132, 134, 138, 139, 141, 143, 147, 149, 150, 151, 156, 159, 164, 167, 169, 173, 174

TELCO, 40, 41, 42, 48, 56, 58, 59, 60, 65, 67, 68, 80, 81, 82, 86, 91, 101, 104, 111, 117, 118, 127

Tengku Ariff Bendahara, 81, 82

Textile, 115, 169

TGTC, 67, 68

TISCO, 1, 5, 6, 7, 8, 9, 11, 12, 13, 15, 16, 17, 18, 19, 21, 22, 25, 29, 32, 34, 39, 40, 41, 42, 43, 44, 45, 47, 48, 49, 51, 53, 91, 93, 101, 102, 175, 176, 177, 180

TLT, 111, 112, 113

TPI, 24, 58, 59, 60, 62, 64, 65, 66, 67, 69, 70, 71, 72, 73, 74, 75, 76, 77, 78, 79, 81, 82, 84, 86, 87, 88, 89, 91, 92, 94, 95, 99, 101, 103, 174, 177

trade restrictions, 106

transmission line towers, 102, 107, 112

TZL, 126, 131, 132, 134, 139, 140, 141, 142, 143

Vivekananda, Swami, 154, 155

World Bank, 6, 148

Young, Nick, 60, 63

Zambia International Business Advisory Council (ZIBAC), 172

Zambia Model, 144

ZIBAC, 172